BIBLE CODE III

BIBLE
CODE III
SAVING THE WORLD

MICHAEL DROSNIN

—

WORLDMEDIA

For my family,
For my friends,
For all who kept the faith,
Again.

"I do not know with what weapons World War III will be fought, but World War IV will be fought with sticks and stones."

— ALBERT EINSTEIN

"Everything is foreseen, but freedom of action is granted."

— THE TALMUD

CONTENTS

INTRODUCTION

BIBLE CODE III is a final warning. These are the predictions we need to survive.

Armageddon is not a myth about another world, a distant time, an imagined final battle, just words for a sermon, or tales in an ancient book.

It is here and now. And you need not be religious to know it. It is not just in the Bible, or its code. It is in the headlines on the front page of every newspaper and the images on every television screen.

But the subtitle of this new book is "Saving the World."

That is because we are at a critical moment in human history—if our world were not in danger there would be no need to save it. But none of the dangers must become our reality.

The Bible Code tells us all our possible futures, not one pre-determined future. The predictions are warnings that allow us to prevent the worst dangers we face. We decide.

In every religion there are a few zealots who misread ancient texts not as prophecy, but as orders to kill, destroy, even to bring the world to an end, in the name of God.

Al Qaeda is the most obvious example. But it is Osama bin Laden —not Islam—that led to 9/11.

Our best weapon against all the zealots is the truth. We can only prevent the dangers we first recognize.

Some have urged me not to tell what the Bible Code predicts, as if by staying silent we will remain safe. But all history shows otherwise. Denying real danger is what leads to disaster.

We cannot wait for a miracle to fall from the sky. The Bible Code may be the miracle we need, all the help we are likely to get. And it's a miracle proven real by modern science.

I am secular, so I call it instead a phenomenon we do not yet fully understand—the future foretold, the news reported from 3000 years ago.

I am just a reluctant fortune-teller, a reporter who finds the code is far more often right than I am.

I have two certainties. The code is real, so we ignore it at our peril. What we do with it will determine our fate.

BIBLE CODE III

OBAMA

ON MAY 28, 2008, six months before the election, I sent Barack Obama a letter through Oprah Winfrey stating three predictions:

"(1) You will win the Democratic nomination and become President;

"(2) You may, as a result of your victories, be assassinated but that danger can be prevented;

"(3) You can, as President, prevent an otherwise nearly certain nuclear terror attack."

"It comes from a source that predicted you would be President before the first vote was cast in Iowa," I told Obama citing the first primary on January 3, when he was practically unknown and given no chance.

"I am sending you this letter through your friend Oprah Winfrey because it may not reach you through regular channels," I wrote. "Also Oprah knows me and she knows the source of my information.

"A world-famous Israeli mathematician has discovered a code in the Bible that predicts events that happened thousands of years after the Bible was written."

On November 4, 2008 the first of the three predictions came true.

Barack Obama became the first African-American to be elected President of the United States, an historic and improbable event that was encoded in the Bible more than 3000 years ago.

Obama's victory was new, dramatic confirmation of the reality of the Bible Code, the secret text hidden in the Old Testament that reveals the future.

"I cannot explain how," I wrote Obama. "I am not religious.

"But I believe the code for the same reason many top intelligence officials do—it keeps coming true."

The code had already predicted the elections of Bill Clinton and George Bush. It had already predicted the assassinations of both John and Robert Kennedy, and Israeli Prime Minister Yitzhak Rabin. Every detail of September 11, 2001 was encoded in the ancient text. The rise of Osama Bin Laden, the fall of Saddam Hussein, both Gulf Wars, were all in the code.

Everything, from World War II to Watergate, from the Holocaust to Hiroshima, from the Great Depression to the current global economic crisis, was encoded in the Bible.

And now, with Obama's historic election, the first of the three predictions found almost a year earlier had also come true.

"If there is anyone out there who still doubts that America is a place where all things are possible," the President-Elect told a hundred thousand people gathered in a park on the waterfront in Chicago, "tonight is your answer."

"I was never the likeliest candidate for this office," Obama said. And yet it was predicted thousands of years ago.

So while I watched his victory, the first prediction, I worried about the danger of his assassination, the second. And I was yet more worried about the third and most terrible prediction, that we might face the real Armageddon, nuclear terror, while he was President.

The Apocalypse. Armageddon. I could hardly believe it myself. As I told Obama, I'm not religious. I don't believe in God. I'm a totally secular, skeptical investigative reporter. I started out on the night police beat at the Washington Post, I covered financial news at the Wall Street Journal, and I still have a down-to-earth sense of reality. So although I wrote a book that made the Bible Code known to the world a dozen years ago, I still woke up every morning not wanting, not quite able to believe the code is real.

But I woke up the morning of November 5 once more certain there is a code in the Bible that reveals the future.

I looked at the code matrixes that predicted Obama's election when no one, including myself, could imagine it was possible.

○ IN 5769 = NOVEMBER 2008   △ OBAMA   ◇ ELECTED   □ PRESIDENT

The table was perfect. "Obama" "elected" "President," and the Biblical
year, "5769," November 2008 in the modern calendar.

Obama won Iowa, just as the code predicted. And the code also said that
a black man would be "President of the United States."

○ OBAMA

○ IOWA

□ HIS TIME

○ PRESIDENT OF THE UNITED STATES   □ BLACK

△ OBAMA

And yet it was inconceivable when we found the prediction in December 2007. Hillary Clinton was ahead by 30 points in every poll, and Obama was black and barely known. But the code stated his victory, in the first primary and the November election.

Clinton and McCain were not even in the race, not in the code. Only Obama. It declared him President before anyone had voted.

The Bible Code did not predict the obvious. Again and again it predicted what no one believed possible—and then it came true.

○ B. OBAMA IS PRESIDENT   △ OBAMA   □ PRESIDENT   ▽ HESHVAN = NOVEMBER

Again the code matrix was perfect. "B. Obama is President" with his name a second time just below, "President" also repeated and the Biblical month of the election "Heshvan," November.

When it happened, on November 4, it was a miracle, actually two miracles. An African-American had been elected President. And the Bible Code had predicted it almost a year in advance—in a text that was 3000 years old.

———

I FIRST HEARD about the Bible Code more than 15 years ago. I had just met with the chief of Israeli intelligence to discuss the future of warfare. As I was leaving the walled military headquarters, the General's aide stopped me.

"There's a mathematician in Jerusalem you should see," he said. "He found the exact day the Gulf War would begin, in the Bible."

"I'm not religious," I said, getting into my car.

"Neither am I," said the soldier. "But he found a code in the Bible with the exact date, three weeks before the war started."

It all seemed beyond belief. I was sure it was crazy. But when I checked out the scientist, I found that he was considered a near genius in the world of mathematics. A professor at Hebrew University, he was the leading expert in the field of math that underlies quantum physics. I went to see him.

With his full beard and yarmulke, Eliyahu Rips looked like a character straight out of the Old Testament. It confirmed all my doubts. Genius or not, this scientist was surely deluded by his religious beliefs. I challenged him to show me the Gulf War in his Bible. Instead, he led me into his small study, turned on his computer, pointed to the screen, and said, "The Bible is a computer program."

"Saddam Hussein" and "Scud missiles" were encoded in the Bible with the exact day Iraq attacked Israel, January 18, 1991.

"How many dates did you find?" I asked. "Just this one, three weeks before the war started," he replied.

"But who knew 3000 years ago that there would be a Gulf War, let alone that a missile would be fired on January 18th?" I asked.

"God," said Rips.

It only made me more skeptical. I asked Rips to look for modern, even future events he had not already found.

We found "President Kennedy" with "Dallas." We found "Bill Clinton" with "President"—six months before he was elected. We found one thing after another encoded in the Bible, things that Rips did not know I would ask him. Eventually, we found several events before they happened—like the collision of a comet with the planet Jupiter, with the name of the comet and the exact date of impact.

The Bible Code kept coming true. A top American code-breaker confirmed it. Famous mathematicians in Israel and the United States, at Harvard, Yale, and Hebrew University, said it was real. Rips' experiment passed three peer reviews at a respected U.S. mathematics journal. But still I could not believe it—until, two years later, I found a code that persuaded even me.

O YITZHAK RABIN   ☐ ASSASSIN WILL ASSASSINATE

On September 1, 1994, I flew back to Israel and met in Jerusalem with a close friend of Prime Minister Yitzhak Rabin. I gave him a letter which he immediately gave to the Prime Minister.

"I have uncovered information that suggests your life is in danger," my letter to Rabin stated. "The only time your full name—'Yitzhak Rabin'—is encoded in the Bible, the words 'assassin that will assassinate' cross your name."

A year later, on November 4, 1995, came the awful confirmation, a shot in the back from a man who believed he was on a mission from God, the murder encoded in the Bible 3000 years ago.

When I heard the news, all the air went out of me. I sunk to the floor, and said out loud, "Oh my God, it's real."

But as great as the shock was on November 4, 1995, it was yet greater on September 11, 2001.

◯ TWIN   ◇ TOWERS   ◇ AIRPLANE

"Twin Towers" was encoded in the ancient text. "Airplane" also appeared, in exactly the same place. "It knocked down" "twice" ran across "airplane" and "towers."

I saw it all happen from the roof of my home in New York, and again said out loud, "Oh my God, it's real."

And if the Bible Code was real, it could have only one purpose—to warn the world of a terrible, even terminal danger. And the danger must be right upon us or we would not be finding the Bible Code now.

For 15 years I have been warning world leaders that an ancient prophecy was about to come true, that the Apocalypse foretold by all the West's three major religions was encoded in the Bible, that nuclear terror was the greatest danger we now faced.

The Bible Code warns that we are right now in the "End of Days," something I can barely even imagine. But I have told three Presidents, Bill Clinton, George Bush, and now Barack Obama.

Are we really, right now, facing the "End of Days"?

———

THE TWO GREAT Biblical Apocalypses, the Book of Daniel in the Old Testament and the Book of Revelation in the New Testament, are predictions of unprecedented horror, to be fully revealed when a secret book is opened at the "End of Days."

In Revelation it is the book "sealed with seven seals" that can be opened only by the Messiah. In Daniel, the original version of the same story, an angel reveals the ultimate future to the Hebrew prophet and then tells him, "But thou, O Daniel, shut up the words, and seal the book until the time of the End."

It was these two verses that caused the first modern scientist, Sir Isaac Newton, to look for a code in the Bible. Newton believed the "sealed book" was the code. He called it "a cryptogram set by the Almighty," the "riddle of the Godhead, the riddle of past and future events divinely fore-ordained."

Three hundred years ago Newton, the man who discovered gravity and figured out the mechanics of our solar system, who single-handedly invented advanced mathematics, searched for a hidden code in the Bible that would reveal the future of mankind.

For more than three thousand years, ever since there's been a Bible, people have believed there was something hidden in it, great secrets that were known only to the high priests, new revelations that could be found using some esoteric formula, some form of magic, some new science.

But it remained for a Russian immigrant to Israel, Eliyahu Rips, a mathematician freed from a Soviet political prison, to find the code that had eluded everyone for millennia.

Rips succeeded because he had the essential tool that everyone before him lacked—a computer.

The Bible Code had a time-lock. It could not be opened until the computer was invented.

It was designed, apparently by some intelligence that could see the future, to be opened now. It was made to allow us to crack the code at this one moment in human history.

"That is why Isaac Newton could not do it," said Rips. "It had to be opened with a computer. It was 'sealed until the time of the End.'"

Rips discovered the Bible Code in the original Hebrew version of the Old Testament, the Bible as it was first written, the words that the Bible itself said God gave to Moses on Mount Sinai 3200 years ago.

Rips eliminated all the spaces between the words, and turned the entire original Bible into one continuous letter strand, 304,805 letters long.

In doing that, he was restoring the Bible to what ancient sages say was its original form. According to legend, it was the way Moses received the Bible from God—"contiguous, without break of words."

Rips wrote a computer program that searched the long string of letters for new information, revealed by skipping any equal number of letters.

Anyone could make up a sentence that would tell one story on the surface, but another story hidden in a simple skip code. For example:

Rips explained that each code is a case of adding every fifth or tenth or fiftieth letter to form a word.

Now read that same sentence as a four-letter skip code:

Rips Expl**A**ine**D** tha**T** eac**H** cod**E** is a **C**ase **O**f ad**D**ing **E**very fifth or tenth or fiftieth letter to form a word.

The hidden message—"**READ THE CODE.**"

But no one, not even Newton, could go through the whole Bible counting letters by hand. Only a computer can search fast enough, and find the complexly interwoven information in the Bible Code.

The words form a crossword puzzle. Each time a new word or phrase is discovered, a new crossword puzzle is formed. Time after time related words, names, dates, and places, detailed information about modern events, are encoded together.

It's what makes the Bible Code unique. In another book one might find a random skip sequence that spells "Barack Obama"—but not with "President." One might find the month of the election—but not with "Obama is President." One might find "Atomic Holocaust" or "World War"—but not with "the End of Days."

"Only in the Bible Code is there consistent, coherent, accurate information, appearing far against the odds," said Rips. "No one has found anything like that in any other book, in any translation, or in any original Hebrew text, except the Bible."

When Rips reported his discovery in an American mathematics journal, many scientists were skeptical. They couldn't fault his science, but they couldn't believe his results. The claim was just too amazing—a code in the Bible that revealed events that happened after the Bible was written.

A senior code-breaker at the top secret National Security Agency, the clandestine U.S. government listening post near Washington, heard about the startling claim, and decided to investigate.

Harold Gans had spent his life making and breaking codes for American military intelligence, and he was sure the Bible Code was "off-the-wall, ridiculous."

He wrote his own computer program, and set out to prove it was a hoax. Instead, his 440-hour experiment proved it was real. "It sent a chill up my spine," recalled the code-breaker.

No man could have encoded the Bible with information about people who lived, events that happened, thousands of years after the Bible was written. But someone did.

If not one of us, then who?

BEFORE CHRISTMAS 2007, before the first vote was cast in the 2008 Presidential election, when there were still nine Democrats in the race, I searched the Bible Code for the winner.

The prediction was a surprise.

I called Professor Rips at his home in Jerusalem and told him that the code had just named the next President of the United States.

"Hillary Clinton?" asked Rips.

"No," I replied. "A young black man named Barack Obama."

"Who is he?" asked Rips.

"I really don't know much about him, but it looks very clear in the code," I said.

The matrix predicted "Obama will be elected," that was crossed by "prophet," but it also predicted something else.

O OBAMA WILL BE ELECTED   □ PROPHET   △ HE WAS ASSASSINATED

Rips saw it immediately, just as I had—"he was assassinated."

"I'm not worried," I told Rips, "because I don't believe that America will actually elect a black President."

But on January 3, 2008 Obama won the first primary in Iowa, shocking everybody, especially Hillary Clinton. On Super Tuesday, a 24 state primary on February 5, Obama and Clinton split the vote.

Suddenly Barack Obama was a serious candidate. And not long after, the New York Times, in a front page story raised the unspoken fear that he would be assassinated.

"HUSHED WORRY ABOUT OBAMA," read the headline. It revealed that Secret Service agents had been surrounding him for months, the earliest any candidate had ever been protected, and that in his campaign everyone remembered 1968, the year both Martin Luther King and Bobby Kennedy were assassinated just two months apart.

The story in the Times eliminated my fear of making the danger public, and it also sent me back to the Bible Code to search for information that might help save the Senator's life.

Working with Rips, I found that Obama's victory and the danger were encoded over and over again, each time against odds of at least a million to one.

"It is clearly intentional," said Rips. "This could not appear repeatedly by chance."

Not since I found the warning that Prime Minister Rabin might be killed had the assassination of any world leader been so clearly encoded in the Bible.

O BARACK OBAMA △ PRESIDENT ▽ ASSASSIN ☐ IN CAPITAL ☐ DEATH

The only time Obama's full name appeared anywhere in the Bible, "President" and "assassin" and "in capital" also did.

And just below "Barack Obama" the same code matrix said "death."

The danger was so clearly encoded, with every step in Obama's remarkable rise to power, it worried me.

When the fireworks went off after he accepted the Democratic nomination before 80,000 people at a football stadium in Denver, I feared it was the sound of gunfire.

When Obama left his armored limousine, and walked the parade route to the White House after his Inauguration, I again feared for his life. Even CNN openly stated the danger.

In his Inaugural address Obama was blunt about dangers America and the world faced: "Every so often the oath is taken amidst gathering clouds and raging storms," he said. "The challenges we face are real. They are serious and they are many."

He cited the economic crisis, the terrorist threat, but there was one danger Obama did not mention—his own assassination.

"Now that the first prediction has come true, now that Obama is President, we must pay attention to the second prediction," said Professor Rips. "They are intertwined."

O PRESIDENT OF THE UNITED STATES □ BLACK
◇ OBAMA   ▽ TIME OF THE MURDER

"Time of murder" crossed "Obama" and "black" "President," just as "Obama will be elected" appeared with "he was assassinated."

Nearly every time the code said Obama would be elected or would be President, it also said he might be killed.

But I was certain that if Obama was actually in danger, his assassination could be prevented.

I did not have one clear date or place—all were probabilities.

But I did have details that would tell the Secret Service who to look for, and how an assassination was likely to happen.

Obviously, I will not reveal the details here. That would help a potential killer, rather than help protect Obama.

But if the code is right, it might help identify the assassin, and allow the Secret Service to do what it had never been able to do before—stop an assassin before he could shoot.

The Bible Code had actually named Rabin's assassin. "Amir,"

His killer, appeared with "name of the assassin," and the one encoding of "Yitzhak Rabin."

Indeed, Israeli intelligence had the killer's name on a list. Unfortunately, Rabin's security detail did not know he was the assassin—until the Prime Minister was dead.

If the Israelis had shared the list, we could have identified the assassin long before the murder.

Perhaps the Secret Service also had a list that named Obama's potential assassin. If so, it would be in the code.

I could not let another world leader die.

———

IN MARCH 2008, I called Valerie Jarrett, Obama's closest friend and top advisor. During the campaign, she was the one person who could go past everyone to the candidate.

I told her about the code, about its warning that Obama might be in danger, and that the same code had predicted Rabin's murder a year in advance.

כ ס ה ה ג ב ו ל מ נ ג ב ל ע מ ה ל ע ק ר ב י ס ע ו ע ב ר
ע ו ה ה י ק ר ת י ס ל כ ס ע ר י ס ו א י ר י מ ק ל ט ה ת ה י
ה ה ד ב ר א ש ר צ ו ה י ה ו ה י ה ו ל ב נ ו ת צ ל פ ח ד ל
ד ה ר ה א מ ר א ש י ה ו ה י ל א י ע י ו נ ת ו נ ל נ
ב ר י ס ב ג ו ל א ח י כ כ ב נ י ע ש ו ה י ש ב י ס
י א ו ל כ ל ע מ ו ל מ ה ל ח מ ה י ה צ ה ו ה נ ת י ו ה י ה
ס ה כ ל ה א כ ה ל י ו ש ע י ה ש י ה ו ל כ ל ה מ מ ל כ ו ת א
ב נ י ת כ ל ר מ ש ב א ד מ ה ב ת נ י ב ת כ ל ד ג ה ה א ש
ש ל נ ס י ה ש מ ה ו ר ו ח צ י ר ש א ר ו ר צ ח א ת ר ע ה ו
ת כ ב ד ת י א נ ת ג ד ל ו ד ל א ת ק ל ו ש מ ע נ ו ו מ ת ו
ח ר ל א מ ר ה מ ה ע ד ו ת ת ו ח י ק ס ו ה מ ו ש פ ט י ס ם
נ י י ה ס ג א ת ה צ ר ע ה א ת צ ע ה י ש ל ח ה ו י א ל א י
ו ב צ ת ב ש מ י ס ע ע מ י ד ג ו ר ו ל ר ס ב נ ע י ק י
ת כ ס ת ו נ פ ל נ פ י ע י ו ה א ת א ר ב א ת ע י ה ס ה
י ז י י ו ש י ו ת ר מ ש מ ר ת ו ו י ח ק ת י ו ר ו מ ש פ ה י
ו א ל מ צ ו ת י ה ו א ל א ו י ו ה ר א כ ס מ כ ש ר א ב ע צ מ
ב ש ע ר י ד ר י ש ד א ו ח מ מ ש ת ל פ נ י י ו ה א ל י ד ב ב כ
י ד ה מ ה צ א ת מ א נ ת א ר מ צ ר ע מ ס י ב מ ת ע ת ד ב ע ד י
ב ו נ ת ו ה ת ה כ ס כ ב ל א ש ר ת א ה נ ו ה פ ש נ ד ב ב
פ ס ח ל י ה ר ו א ל א י כ צ ב ח ב כ ש ד ה ב א י ב ה ה ו
א ו ת א ה ש ה ו ס ק ל ת ס ב א נ ב ס י ת מ ר ו ת מ ע ו
ת ה א ל ה ר ת ו א ל א י ד ר ו מ ש א ו ת ס ר ה מ ת ס ה נ פ ב
א ש ר י ס ה ד י ת ו ר ה ד ו ה מ ת ד ו ש ר ש י ט פ ש ו ט פ ב
ש ו ה נ י ס נ ה כ נ י ג ל י ו ל י כ ר ב ס ח ד ב ר י ה ו ו א
א ל א ה ה ז ה ר ע א ת ר ש ת ז ר ה א ת ב א ת ה כ ה ה ר כ ל א
ל ת ו ד ה מ ח ה י ה ו ה י ה ל נ ו פ ת ו י ר ע ת ב ר צ ח ב
י ת מ ו א ב ו ת ע ל ב י ס י נ ב ו י ס נ ב ל א י ו מ ת

Jarrett promised to give Obama a letter from me. But the day before she met with him the Rev. Wright scandal broke. A video of Obama's pastor shouting "God damn America!" played over and over again on national television. I knew my letter would not reach the candidate anytime soon.

But Jarrett did send my letter to the chief of his protective detail. However, no one at the Secret Service would meet with me, or look at the evidence, although the warning had come from the top of Obama's campaign.

So, in May 2008 I contacted Oprah. She had helped launch the Obama campaign, drawing huge crowds for him before he could do it himself, and I had been on her show when my first Bible Code book was published.

Through Oprah I again sent a letter to Obama. It stated the three predictions, including his election, and the danger of his assassination.

But it also emphasized he could be saved.

"I have information that your life might be in danger," I opened my letter to Obama, "but also detailed information that may help protect you."

○ OBAMA WILL BE ELECTED   △ ASSASSINATED
⬠ LIST   ☐ BLOCKED   ○ SAVING

The code said Obama could be saved.

A matrix that warned Obama might be killed, also said the murder could be prevented.

It was the same encoding Professor Rips and I had found almost a year before the election, that predicted both Obama's victory and his assassination.

But now I saw that "saving" also appeared.

The code actually suggested how the murder could be "blocked"— by using a "list" of suspects, just as the Israelis could have to save Rabin.

When I next spoke to Jarrett, she had already heard from Oprah, and she immediately contacted the Secret Service. Jarrett now sent the head of Obama's protective unit detailed information from the Bible Code.

Finally, a top Secret Service official, Richard K. Elias, the Assistant Director for Intelligence, spoke to me by telephone. I told him what I had just told Jarrett.

"You might already have the name of Obama's assassin on a list, but not know it," I said. "If you share your list of suspects, we might be able to identify him in the code."

Elias refused. But he assured me that everyone, at Secret Service headquarters in Washington, and everyone protecting Obama in the field had the information I sent through Jarrett.

He had clearly read my memo carefully, he noted each of the key details, who might attempt an assassination, and how.

I realized that just by being on alert, by focusing on a profile of the assassin stated in the code, the Secret Service may have already prevented an attack. Still, I remained concerned.

"The Secret Service has never once prevented an assassination," I said. "Every time a man with a gun has gotten within a range of a President, he's been shot, usually killed."

Elias did not deny it. He just said, "We're way better now."

And Elias and I both knew the danger was not over. It could not be more clearly stated in the code.

ע ה ו ו ו נ ב ר ז ע ל א ת א ו ן ר ה ה א ת א ח ק ה ב י ר מ י מ
ח י פ ל ל א ר ש י י ה כ י י ל א ר ש י ב ס ח ל י י ה צ ה י
א י ו ק ל ב ל א ו א ב י ו (ב) א ו מ י ו ש ו מ ו ק י ו ס כ מ
ב ו מ א י ו ד ד ב כ ל כ ו (א) א ל ס נ מ א ה י ל א ת כ ל ה ה א
א ק ל ב ו מ א י ו ה ש ע א (ו) ת א * ו ה י ו ב ד י ו ש א ל כ
ל כ א י ו ן ה י ◇ ל א י ח (ב) ז ל ס ע ל ן א ו ק ת ו ב א ו מ
ו ז ל י י נ י כ י ה ת ⟨ח⟩ פ ש (מ) ן י כ י ל י י נ י מ י ה ת ה פ ש
ו ב ח ה ת ח פ ש מ ו ב ח ◇(ה) ע י ו ב י נ ב ל י י ע י י ר ב ה ה ת
ח א ל ו ת ל ח נ ת א ס ת ת (נ)◇ ת ב ו ל ן י א ס א ו ו נ ב ל
ו ל י א ל ן י ה ה ת ש י ל (ש) ו ר ◇ ל ה י ה י ן י ה ה י צ ח
ו ק ב י נ ב ס י ו פ * ו ה (ו) ל ח ח י ⟨כ⟩ ח י ה ר ה ש א ה ל ע ס
ו ס א ו ה ו ד נ ת א ה י ב (א) ע מ ש ו ה י ⟨ל⟩ ע נ ב ה י ב א ת
ח ה י ד ו ק פ ל ע ה ש מ ף צ ק י ו ה נ ח מ ל ◇ ו ח מ ל א ס
ח ו ף ל א ס י ש ל ש ו ה ש ש ו ק ב ו ת ו א מ ש מ ◇ו ס י פ
ב ה ס א ו ש א ד ע ל א ו ש י י נ ב י נ פ ל ס י ש ח צ ל ח נ
ח ל ס ו י ו ש ע [ה] ש [מ] ח [ב] ו [ן] ש [א] ו ה ש ד ח ב ס ס מ ע ו מ
ש ה ל ב א ד ע ת מ ש י ה ת י ב מ ן ד ו י ה ל ע ו נ ח י ו ו
י נ ב ל י ל ג י י ן ב י ק ב [א] ⟨ש⟩ [נ] ו ד י נ ב ה ט מ ל ו ו נ
ה ו י ב ה ד ע ה ו ט פ ש ו נ ת ע ר ש ק ב מ א ל ו ו ב י ו
נ ב ל א ה ש מ ד י ב * ו ה י ה ו צ ר ש א ס י ט פ ש מ ה ו ת

○ B. OBAMA IS PRESIDENT   △ OBAMA   □ PRESIDENT

◇ IN RETURN, HE WAS ASSASSINATED

"B. Obama is President," the only time it was encoded in the Bible, was crossed in the same matrix by "in return, he was assassinated."

"The closer Obama gets to the White House the more danger he is in," I said. "And it will not end if Obama is elected."

Elias agreed. He said the Secret Service had come to the same conclusion as the Bible Code—Barack Obama would be in danger even as President of the United States.

In fact, after Obama became President the threats to kill him received by the Secret Service jumped 400 percent.

The atmosphere of right-wing rage only increased.

In the summer of 2009 protesters openly carrying weapons came to town hall meetings on the health care bill. In April 2010 there was an armed march on Washington, with demonstrators carrying guns and racist signs.

The New York Times, the Washington Post, television commentators all talked openly about the danger of assassination.

I did not publish the code's prediction of Rabin's assassination until after he was murdered. That allowed Israeli intelligence and the Prime Minister himself to ignore the warning.

I cannot again wait. The way to prevent Obama's assassination is to publish in advance the repeated warnings in the Bible Code, not to allow the White House and the Secret Service to ignore the danger.

It raises again the question that has come up so many times when the code predicts a great danger.

If the future is known, can it be changed?

I was certain it could be. Nothing in the Bible Code is written in stone. The code tells every possible future, not one pre-determined future. In fact, I think the code exists to allow us to change our future.

"Everything the code states is a probability," I wrote Obama in the letter I sent him through Oprah. "We, using our free will, determine what actually happens."

President Obama can be saved.

But can he save the world from a danger so great it is only captured by the words of Biblical prophecy?

CHAPTER TWO

NUCLEAR TERROR

AL QAEDA ALREADY has nuclear weapons.

In fact, the Bible Code reveals exactly where, a dot in the desert first named in the code that Israeli satellites have confirmed is an Al Qaeda base.

While I was trying to alert the White House, to prevent the annihilation of New York, Washington, and Israel, President Barack Obama was holding a 47-nation nuclear security summit, the biggest meeting of world leaders in Washington since the United Nations was created.

"Terrorist networks such as Al Qaeda have tried to acquire the material for a nuclear weapon," Obama said in his opening speech to the world leaders in April 2010, "and if they ever succeed, they would surely use it."

What the President did not know was that months earlier Israel's top intelligence analyst had told Obama's top counter-terrorism advisor that he had satellite photographs of a remote Al Qaeda base no one had ever before seen, that the Bible Code stated was the hide-out for nuclear weapons.

But American intelligence has made no effort to look at the terrorist base, to find the weapons, or capture them.

The matrix in the code that reveals the future told who, what, when, and where against odds of 100 million to 1. The odds of Israel confirming every detail were incalculable.

"Bible Code" appeared with "Bin Laden" and "atomic" and stated an exact time frame of the danger—"starting 2006" and ending "2011."

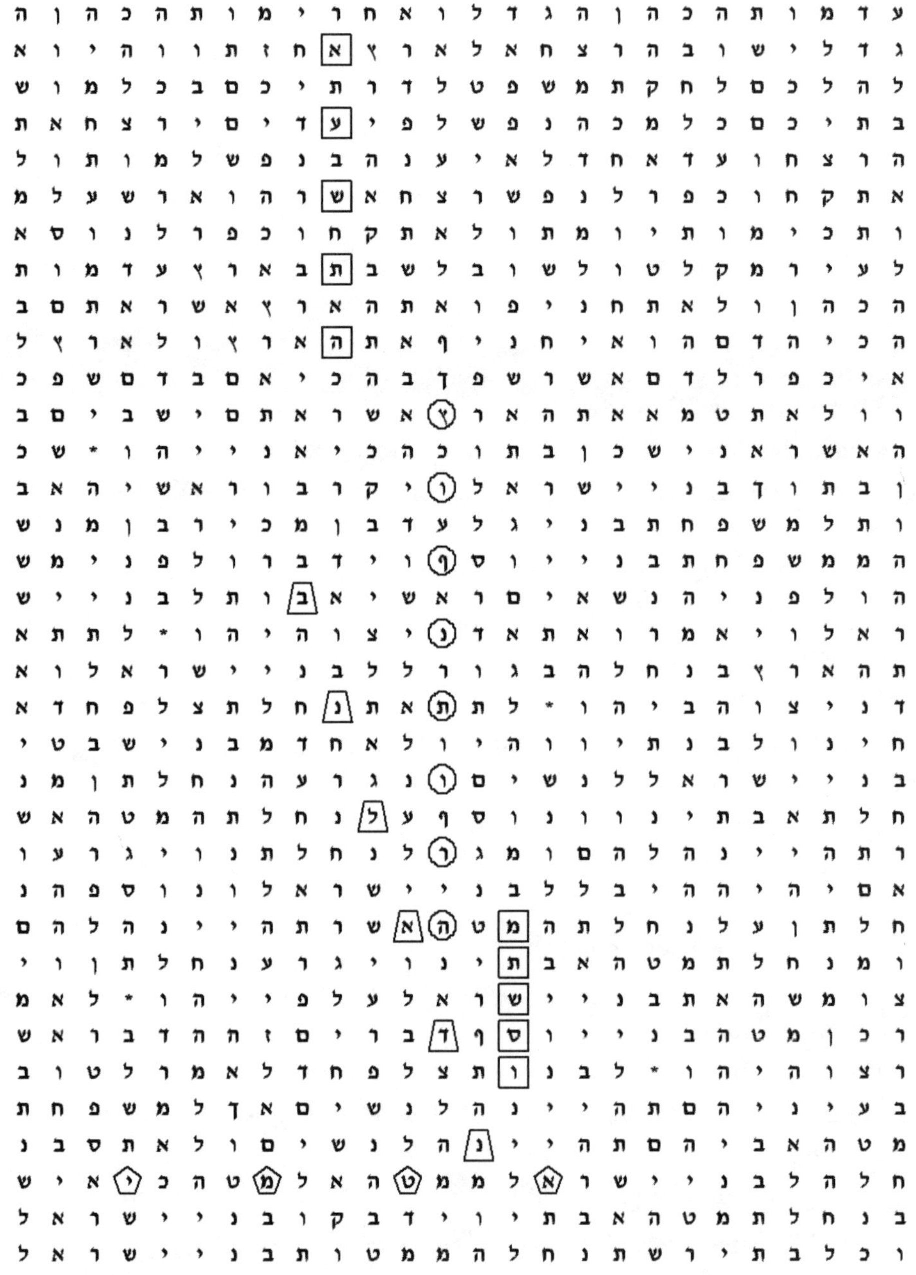

○ BIBLE CODE △ BIN LADEN ⬠ ATOMIC □ STARTING 5766 / 2006

□ 5771 / 2011

When the President warned the world of the urgent need to secure or destroy nuclear weapons and materials at the summit, Al Qaeda may already have had nuclear weapons for four years.

And if we do not prevent it now, there may be a nuclear terror attack next year.

It was the third prediction I sent Obama through Oprah — "You can, as President, prevent an otherwise nearly certain nuclear terror attack."

At his summit Obama said, "Just the smallest amount of plutonium—about the size of an apple—could kill and injure hundreds of thousands of innocent people."

"Nuclear materials that could be sold or stolen and fashioned into a nuclear weapon exist in dozens of nations."

But Obama did not know that he was trying to close the barn door after the horses had already escaped.

In fact, the same code matrix that stated the danger also clearly stated the entire nightmare.

The Bible Code that linked "Bin Laden" to "Atomic" was crossed by a chilling statement: "In Yemen for terrorism, and Khan built."

A.Q. Khan was the Pakistani scientist who built his country's nuclear weapons by stealing the technology from Western Europe, and then went into business for himself.

Khan sold nuclear designs and technology, indeed whole bomb factories, to the world's most dangerous countries—Iran, North Korea, and Libya—through a global nuclear black market.

And here the code stated that Khan also sold or gave nuclear weapons to Osama Bin Laden.

In fact, the very White House advisor, John Brennan, who ignored Israel's confirmation of the code, held a press conference at the summit and told reporters of campfire conversations between Bin Laden and two Pakistani nuclear scientists working with Khan in August 2001, right before 9/11.

There is no more dangerous conspiracy possible than the lethal combination of A.Q. Khan, the "father of the Islamic bomb," and Osama Bin Laden.

One had demonstrated his ability to build nuclear weapons, the other had stated that he would use them.

○ BIBLE CODE △ BIN LADEN ⬠ ATOMIC □ STARTING 5766 / 2006

□ 5771 / 2011 ◇ IN YEMEN FOR TERRORISM, AND KHAN BUILT

Indeed, Bin Laden had called for "an American Hiroshima."

But Obama's terror advisor, Brennan, never told the President that the Israelis had confirmed what the Bible Code stated, he never told Obama that he was given the exact location where Al Qaeda might already have nuclear weapons, he refused to see the codes, and he even refused to look at the Israeli satellite photographs.

"Atomic Weapon" is encoded only once in the Bible. In that code matrix the immediate danger of a nuclear terror attack is very clearly stated.

○ ATOMIC WEAPON □ HE LOCATED THERE △ ATOMIC

◇ HE WILL STRIKE IMMEDIATELY

"He will strike immediately" crossed "atomic weapon." And "he located there" was crossed by "atomic."

There were two stark alternatives stated in the code: either we had to strike the terrorists immediately, or the terrorists might strike us as soon as 2011.

I obviously cannot reveal in this book the exact location of Bin Laden's nuclear weapons, clearly stated in the code, because if I do, Al Qaeda will simply move them to a new, unknown location.

But both American and Israeli intelligence know the place stated in the 3000 year old code.

It accurately named one dot in the desert from every place in the world as an Al Qaeda base, and accurately described every structure at the never before seen location, and that was all documented by the Israelis in satellite photographs the White House refused to see.

When Professor Rips and I found the matrix that links "Bin Laden" and "atomic" to the Pakistani nuclear scientist "Khan," the puzzle almost revealed itself, until the whole horrifying picture was before our eyes.

First we found "Bible Code" with "Bin Laden" and "atomic," but "atomic" appeared three more times. Rips saw that once the full encoding stated "father of atomic science." "Who would that be?" he asked me.

"It could be Einstein, it could be Oppenheimer who built our atomic bomb, but in the Islamic world, it would be A.Q. Khan," I said. "In fact, he's

NUCLEAR TERROR   27

known as 'the father of the Islamic bomb.'"

Rips searched for "Khan" in the matrix. "Look at this," he said, pointing at the computer screen. In one unbroken 18-letter strand that crossed "Bin Laden" and "Bible Code" and "atomic" was the 100 million to 1 revelation:

"In Yemen for terrorism, and Khan built."

"This is remarkable," said Rips. "It tells the danger without one wasted word. It is clearly intentional, it could not happen by chance."

The next appearance of "atomic" was equally extraordinary. It crossed "mega-terror attack."

And the final "atomic" was part of a phrase stating "atomic instruction," and it crossed "father of atomic science," and that connected it all to "Yemen," "terrorism," and "Khan."

○ BIBLE CODE   ◻ BIN LADEN   ▽ ATOMIC   ◻ STARTING 2006
○ 2011   ◇ IN YEMEN FOR TERRORISM, AND KHAN BUILT
◇ FATHER OF ATOMIC SCIENCE   ○ ATOMIC INSTRUCTION
◻ MEGA-TERROR ATTACK   ◇ ATOMIC

It was not only beyond chance, it was beyond imagination.

The ultimate danger the world right now faces was encoded in detail, with names, places, and dates, in a 3000 year old text.

And it was all left for us to find, at the only moment in human history we could, when the computer was invented—just when we needed it to survive.

The only real question now is whether President Obama, who brought the world to Washington to combat nuclear terror, can get his own intelligence agencies to finish the job Israel began.

We can capture or destroy the weapons Al Qaeda has right now, and win the first battle of World War III with 30 commandos.

The question is whether we will.

———

IF NOT, THIS can happen tomorrow:

You are awakened by the terrifying news: "A nuclear attack has destroyed Washington, D.C."

The report on your clock radio is the horror everyone knew would eventually happen, the danger stated by every U.S. government panel since 9/11, the predicted Apocalypse encoded in the Bible 3000 years ago.

You hear news so overwhelming that September 11, 2001 becomes a distant memory—". . . believed to be terrorists, possibly a suicide bomber, and the death toll has already passed a million."

In fact, the Bible Code predicts an attack on "America" by "nuclear" "terror", indeed by a "suicide bomber."

On December 1, 2008, a panel of top experts mandated by the 9/11 Commission, published a report, "World at Risk," that confirmed the Bible Code:

"The Commission believes that unless the world community acts decisively and with great urgency, it is more likely than not that a weapon of mass destruction will be used in a terrorist attack somewhere in the world by the end of 2013."

For fifteen years I have been trying to warn everyone from the President on down of the danger. I told George W. Bush a month before 9/11, and warned him again a month later: "Last time we lost two tall buildings and 3000 people. Next time we may lose an entire city."

Imagine it. Washington has been wiped out. Our entire government is annihilated. The White House is ground zero.

That, too, is predicted in the code.

○ THE WHITE HOUSE   □ ATOMIC   ◇ SUICIDE BOMBER

⏢ ATOMIC DISASTER   ▽ TERRORISM

"White House" is encoded with "atomic" "suicide bomber" in the ancient text of the Bible.

If it happens—and every expert on nuclear terrorism agrees that an American city will be annihilated, if we don't act right now to prevent it—the world would change forever.

What really worries the experts is exactly what the code warns would come next. "Atomic Holocaust," "World War," both encoded with the "End of Days."

The question, according to every expert, is when, not if.

It really could happen. Washington, or any major city in the world, might be destroyed tomorrow by terrorists armed with nuclear weapons.

"A single cell worked for six years to prepare for the hijacking of the American jumbo jets that would attack the World Trade Center and the Pentagon," wrote Graham Allison, Assistant Secretary of Defense for both Clinton and Reagan.

"If a similar cell is now in its fifth or sixth year of preparation for a nuclear terrorist attack, we may not know until a mushroom cloud engulfs an American city."

Picture the horror:

There would be no television images after the first awful flash of light, but we know that hell would follow.

The whole city would be flattened instantly. Fires set by the nuclear blast would gather into a firestorm, one huge fireball miles wide. A violent whirlwind created by the explosion would sweep through the ruins of the city. The fire and the winds would last hours. The radiation would spread for miles and last for years.

The details would probably never be known. The terrorists, the bomb, and the city would all vanish in seconds. But Washington most likely would be destroyed by a weapon like the 12.5 kiloton atomic bomb we dropped on Hiroshima in 1945. Now that would be merely a tactical nuclear weapon, small enough to be carried in a backpack by a "Shaheed," a suicide bomber.

And a nuclear bomb exploded on the ground would create an even greater horror than the Hiroshima bomb. The entire population of Washington would be instantly reduced to dust, any human being in the city would be smoke and ashes. They would simply disappear. The incinerated population would rise up into the mushroom cloud that had been Washington, D.C.

No one in the city would hear the huge explosion because a nuclear blast would create a vacuum. But miles away everyone would hear the terrible thunder, unlike anything they had ever heard before.

Satellite images would finally reveal the devastation.

No one would be left alive. The President, all of Congress, everyone in every major government agency would be reduced to radioactive dust. Not a building would be left standing. Washington would cease to exist.

In the next few days the radiation and the growing firestorm would consume everything and everyone within miles from ground zero. There would be nothing but the burnt-out shells of what was once the capital of the United States.

And that would not be the ultimate horror.

The Bible Code predicts that World War III may start this way. A nuclear attack on Washington or New York would be the beginning, not the end.

———

How can we prevent religious fanatics from destroying the world in the name of God? We need a miracle.

Perhaps the Bible Code is the miracle. It foretold the danger long before 9/11, long before nearly anyone could even imagine terrorism on that scale.

"Instead of a nuclear war between superpowers the world may now face a new threat—terrorists armed with nuclear weapons," I wrote in my first Bible Code book published in 1997.

"World War II ended with an atomic bomb. World War III may start that way."

O WORLD WAR   △ SUICIDE BOMBER   ▽ TERRORISM   □ WAR TO KNIFE

If the Bible Code is right, a "suicide bomber" may trigger the next "World War," the ultimate act of "terrorism."

That was the warning I gave Israeli Prime Minister Shimon Peres in January 1996. When we met again five years later, Peres said, "When I first saw you it was all so hard to believe. Now it's almost ordinary common sense. The world is catching up with the Bible Code."

At first no one but Peres believed what the code predicted. After September 11, 2001, what no one could imagine became what everyone feared.

If Al Qaeda could knock down the Twin Towers, and then hit the Pentagon, armed only with box cutters, no one doubted it might one day attack with nuclear weapons.

"America" is encoded in the Bible twice with "atomic" and "nuclear" and "terror," both times also with "suicide bomber."

O AMERICA   △ ATOMIC   □ SUICIDE BOMBER

The warning of a nuclear terror attack on America is repeated again and again in the Bible Code.

א צ ה ת א ו ק ש ה ו ר א ב ה י פ ל ע מ ו ב א ה ת א
מ ק מ ל ר א ב ה י פ ל ע ו ב א ה ת א ו ב י ש ה י ו ו
י ו ס ת א ו י א מ י ח ⒜ ב ק ע י ס ה ל ה ר מ א י ו ה
ע ד י ה ס ה ל ר מ א י ו נ ח נ א נ ו ח מ ו ר מ א
י ו נ ע ד י ו מ ר א י ו ו ח נ נ ב י ב ל ת א ס ת
ו ס ו ל ש ו ר מ א י ו ו ל ס ו ל ש ה ס ה ל ר מ א י
ו ה ר מ א י ו ו א צ ה ה ⒮ ע ה א ב ו ת ב ל ח ר ה נ ה
ה ה נ ק מ ה ף ס א ה ת ע א ל ל ו ד ג ס ו י ה ד ו ע
כ ו נ א ל ו ר מ א י ו ו ע ר ו כ ל ו ו א צ ה ו ק ש
א ו ל ל ג ו ס י ר ד ע ה ל כ ו פ ס א י ו ש א ד ע ל
ו א צ ה ו נ י ק ש ה ו ⒭ א ב ה י פ ל ע מ ו ב א ה ת
ו א צ ה ס ע ה א ב ל ח ר ו ס מ ע ר ב ד מ ו י ד ו ע
ר ו ש א כ י ה י ו א נ ו ה ה ע ר י כ ה י ב א ל ר ש א
ת א ו ו מ א י ח א נ ו ב ל ת ב ל ח ר ת א ב ק ע י ה א
א ל ג י ו ב ק ע י ש ⟨ג⟩⒤ ו ו מ א י ח א נ ב ל י נ א צ
ב ל ו א צ א ק ש י ו ⟨ד⟩ א ב ה י פ ל ע מ ו ב א ה ה
ת א א ש י ו ל ח ר ל ב ק ⟨ע⟩ י ק ש י ו ו מ א י ח א ו
א י ח א י ו כ ל ח ר ל ב ק ע ⟨י⟩ ד ג י ו ו ז ב י ו ו ל ק
ג ת ו י צ ר ת ו א ה ה ה ⒫ ב ר ⟨ו⟩ ב י כ ו א ו ה ה י ב
ק ע י ע מ ש ת א ו ב ל ע מ ש כ ⟨י⟩ ה י ו ה י ב א ל ר
ו ו ל ק ב ח י ו ו ת א ר ק ל צ ר י ו ו ת ח א נ ב ב
ל ר פ ס י ו ו ת י ב ל א ו ה א י ב י ו ל ק ש י ו י
ל ו ל ו מ א י ו ה ל א ⒣ ס י ר ב ד ה כ ל א נ ב ל
ד ח ו מ ע ב ⟨ש⟩ י ו ה ת א י ר ש ב י ו י מ צ ע ד א נ ב
א י ח א י כ ⟨ה⟩ ב ק ע י ל ל ו ב ל ר מ א י ו ס י מ י ש
ר כ ש מ ה מ ⟨י⟩ ל ה ד ל ג ה ס נ ח י נ ת ד ב ע ו ה ה ת
י ה א ל ⟨ה⟩⟨ל⟩⟨ד⟩⟨ג⟩⟨ה⟩ ס ם ש ת ו נ ב י ת ש ו ב ל ל ו ד ת
ח ר ו ת ו כ ר ה א ל נ י ו ל ח ר ה ר ה נ ט ה ס ש
י ב ה א י ו ה א ר מ ת פ י ו ר א ת ת פ י ה ת י ה ל
ס י י ש ע ב ש ד ד ב א ר מ א י ו ל ח ר ת א ב ק ע

○ AMERICA △ NUCLEAR □ SUICIDE BOMBER □ THE BIG ONE

"America" was crossed by "nuclear," just as it had appeared with "atomic," and again with the Arabic word for "suicide bomber," "Shaheed." The same terrorists who had blown up a bus or a hotel or a train, who attacked on 9/11, would go to greater glory blowing up themselves with an entire city.

Professor Rips, the Israeli scientist who discovered the Bible Code, calculated the odds against it being encoded twice. It was 10 million to 1.

The warning could not be more clear.

Before I warned Obama, long before he became President, I had been in the White House, I had warned both Clinton and Bush, I had sat with the Chief of the Mossad in Israel, I had been in the inner sanctums of the CIA and the Pentagon, met with the entire top command of American military intelligence, and told them all that we might have only a few years left to save our world. But no one would heed the warning.

After 9/11 they all believed me, but no one did anything.

The Chairman of the 9/11 Commission, Governor Thomas Kean, said at the end of 2005, "We have no greater fear than a terrorist who is inside the United States with a nuclear weapon. The consequences of such an attack would be catastrophic. The most striking thing to us is that the size of the problem still totally dwarfs the response."

"We believe that the terrorists will strike again," said the final statement of the full Commission, which issued a report card that gave the Bush administration a failing grade on weapons of mass destruction.

I first warned President Bush more than a month before 9/11, but he ignored my letter, just as he ignored a top secret CIA report he received the same day. It was entitled "Osama bin Laden Determined to Strike U.S. Mainland."

"We need to do today what we would do the day after an entire city is wiped out," I wrote President Clinton in October, 2005, hoping that he, although out of office, could do what Bush, in office, would not. But Clinton would not intervene.

The day after no one would hesitate. We would finally have the will to survive, but perhaps not the way.

If one city is annihilated, every world leader would try to prevent the next city, and the city after that, finally all of human civilization, from being destroyed. But if not now when the world is whole, how could they save the world after it was shattered?

The Bible Code may be a miracle, but it is not like the Bible itself. It is neither a threat of Divine Punishment, nor a promise of Divine Salvation. It is just information, like a news report, but in advance, from 3000 years ago.

We have to use the information in the code to find our own solution, now.

Now, finally, a world leader has appeared who might actually be able to perform the miracle.

Starting in April 2009 Obama tried to sound the alarm.

"The spread of nuclear weapons or the theft of nuclear material could lead to the extermination of any city on the planet," he warned in his first trip abroad as President.

Obama realized the threat had changed. The danger was no longer the danger of the Cold War, missiles flying across the globe, wiping out everything in half an hour. Now it is terrorists armed with weapons of mass destruction.

"In a strange turn of history, the threat of global nuclear war has gone down, but the risk of nuclear attack has gone up," said Obama.

"If Al Qaeda doesn't already have nuclear weapons they're incompetent," a senior CIA official told me at the agency's Langley, Virginia headquarters. "And if they already have a weapon, they could attack today or tomorrow."

"It may take the destruction of a whole city to wake up the world," said Professor Rips. Several leading experts, their repeated warnings ignored, have come to the same conclusion.

It need not be Washington, it may be New York, it may be Jerusalem, it may be Tel Aviv, all are encoded as being in danger, and all could be wiped out in one day.

When I met with the Chief of the Mossad in Israel I showed him that "Jerusalem" was encoded with "atomic" "mega-terror attack," crossed by "Bin Laden" and "war."

○ IN JERUSALEM ◁ MEGA-TERROR ATTACK ◇ ATOMIC ○ BIN LADEN □ WAR

It's too horrifying to imagine, so horrifying that even the men whose job it is to prevent it, instead try to deny it.

When I met with Deputy Director of the CIA I showed him that "New York" was also encoded with "atomic" "mega-terror attack."

"How can you write 'New York' in Hebrew?" he asked.

"The same way you write 'Jerusalem' in English," I replied.

"But how can 'atomic' possibly be written in Hebrew?" he asked.

"Israel has nuclear weapons," I replied.

○ NEW YORK   ⬜ MEGA-TERROR ATTACK   ◇ ATOMIC

Sometimes when I'm home alone in New York, I look at one of the many code matrixes that predict a nuclear terror attack on my own city, and realize that it not only can happen, but that if it happens anywhere it almost certainly will happen in New York, as well as Washington.

I cannot forget the horror of watching the 9/11 attack on the World Trade Towers from the roof of my home just a mile away, and sometimes as I flip through the codes I can see an awful flash of light, and imagine that the entire city is gone.

○ IN NEW YORK   △ OBAMA   ▽ ATOMIC   ☐ 5771 = 2011

"New York" and "atomic" appear together again in the code with "Obama" and "2011." The horror may not be far off.

A nuclear terror attack anywhere in the world will set off a chain reaction of nuclear terror attacks all over the world.

It would almost certainly continue until every major city is destroyed, millions of people murdered by a death cult acting in the name of God. Where once great cities stood, defining the world, its economy, its civilization, there would only be radioactive ruins.

In fact, the Bible Code warns that we might all face an "Atomic Holocaust" before the end of Obama's first term, in 2011.

It would be, as the code warns, an "atomic holocaust for all." The world would change forever, in an instant.

O FOR ALL ATOMIC HOLOCAUST △ 5771 = 2011 ☐ WAR

CAN WE STILL change our future?

"All that the United States and its allies have to do to prevent nuclear terrorism is to prevent terrorists from acquiring a weapon," says the top expert, Graham Allison.

A year before his nuclear summit in Washington, Obama surprised everyone with an historic speech in Prague calling for "a world without nuclear weapons."

But there are 25,000 nuclear weapons in the world, and thousands of terrorists ready to use them. Even Obama said he does not expect to see a world without nuclear weapons in his lifetime.

Russia and the United States have 90% of the weapons. Most are on missiles still pointed at each other, 20 years after the Cold War ended, on 5 minute hair-trigger alert. A false alarm could cause a global catastrophe.

There is no plan to deal with the weapons or enriched uranium in Pakistan, India, or North Korea, and no realistic plan to stop Iran and other countries in the Middle East from also becoming nuclear powers.

Obama's 2010 nuclear summit ended with a call to secure or destroy all nuclear weapons and materials in 4 years, but the 9/11 Commission said we face a nuclear terror attack in 3 years.

Even the 4 year plan would require Russia and China to join the U.S. But it is not clear if France will.

The President is leading, but no one is following.

Even Obama's own counter-terror advisor is making no effort to deal with the most immediate danger, nuclear weapons Al Qaeda may already have at a known base in Yemen. The CIA and the Pentagon are also ignoring the danger. And Obama's Chief of Staff will not look at the evidence, let alone intervene.

It is as if Washington had, in fact, been wiped out. It is as if the American government no longer existed.

President Bush said nuclear terror was the #1 threat, but did nothing to prevent it. Obama has inherited a world at risk.

Osama bin Laden is still on the loose, still threatening "an American Hiroshima." Al Qaeda has attacked London, Madrid, Egypt, and Jordan. It has stated that "eliminating Israel is the duty of every believer."

No one has any idea where to find the terrorists. Our enemy is everywhere. It lives anonymously among us, in every major city, in every major country in the world.

There is no way of knowing whether a nuclear bomb has already been smuggled into Washington, New York, Jerusalem, Tel Aviv, Moscow, London, or Paris, or anywhere else in Europe or Asia, the Middle East or America.

Allison, one of the authors of the report that warned a nuclear attack is likely within 3 years, also stated, "If terrorists bought or stole a nuclear weapon, they could explode it today."

Now, again imagine it is the day after. Washington has been annihilated.

The entire world is in a state of shock. Civilization is rapidly disintegrating. Government offices are abandoned. Hospitals are deserted. There is no food, no fuel, no one to keep order, let alone defend the world.

No one knows when the next bomb will explode, which city might disappear tomorrow.

And in a world now gripped by terror, and in chaos, all the thousands of nuclear weapons would be even more vulnerable, there would be no way to bring them under control.

No one would know where to find the terrorists or how to stop the next attack. An invisible enemy, now armed with nuclear weapons, could knock out one city at a time or five cities at once.

The day after one city was annihilated, everyone would be fleeing every major city, and world leaders would be hiding in underground bunkers.

The day after everyone would wonder how we could have first created weapons that could destroy the world, and then lost control of them, why we let our most dangerous weapons fall into the hands of lunatics, and then did nothing to stop them.

The day after no one would be able to put a shattered world back together.

The day after would be a day too late.

———

OBAMA KNOWS IT, but he came into office facing a world more clearly in crisis then any President since Franklin Roosevelt.

Now, as then, the world economy had crumbled, while at the same time we may face a World War.

I recalled a sealed letter I gave my lawyer in 1998 that made two predictions.

"The warnings that are most clearly stated in the code are:

"(a) The world will face a global 'economic collapse';

"(b) This will lead to a period of unprecedented danger, as nations with nuclear weapons become unstable, and terrorists can buy or steal the power to destroy whole cities."

When I read the predictions ten years later, they shook me. We were already in the moment forecast.

CHAPTER THREE

ECONOMIC CRISIS

It LOOKED LIKE the 1930s all over again, but happening at the warp-speed of the 21st century.

It made the Great Depression seem as if it had happened at an almost leisurely pace. Now all the bad news was global in an instant, and all over the world great economies were falling.

It started in 2008. The U.S. stock market lost half its value, an $8 trillion drop. Flagship corporations of America were at the brink of bankruptcy—General Motors, General Electric, and Citigroup. Unemployment hit a record level, and millions more would be out of work in 2009, even 2010, perhaps 2011.

Are we heading for a yet greater crash in 2012?

It is the danger foretold in the Bible Code. A second Great Depression in 2012.

I had found it in October 2007, a year before the crisis began, when the stock market was at an all-time high, the Dow Jones over 14,000. But I remembered that the market had also peaked right before it crashed in 1929.

"Economic Crisis" was encoded in the Bible just one time. But in exactly the same place "the Depressions" appeared, although it too was in the Bible only once. That was a thousand to 1.

In the same code matrix was the Biblical year "5690," 1929 in the modern calendar, the year of the great crash that triggered the Great Depression. That was 3 in a million.

○ ECONOMIC CRISIS   □ THE DEPRESSIONS   △ IN 1929 / 5690   ◇ 5772 = 2012

Another year also appeared, "5772", in the modern calendar 2012. The code stated this new "economic crisis" would not end, indeed might peak, in Obama's first term. That was a million to 1.

So perhaps it was no accident that it was all encoded exactly where the original words of the Bible told the famous story of Joseph seeing the future by interpreting the Pharaoh's dreams, "seven years of feast and seven years of famine."

The first shock came suddenly in mid-September 2008. The six weeks that followed brought the American economy to its knees, shook the whole world, and made Barack Obama President.

But it also left him facing the worst economic crisis since Roosevelt.

By the time Obama was elected in November everyone knew we were in a crisis, but no one yet imagined how bad it would become.

When Obama was sworn in January 20, 2009 the stock market fell another 5 percent, its biggest drop on any Inauguration Day.

It was an ever escalating disaster on an almost Biblical scale, like the Ten Plagues of Egypt. And it was all encoded in the Bible 3000 years ago.

JUST A YEAR after the Great Recession started, however, almost everyone was saying it was already over.

The Chairman of the Federal Reserve, Ben Bernanke, officially announced it was "very likely" that the recession had ended, that an economic recovery had begun.

In October 2009 the Dow went over 10,000 for the first time in a year. Wall Street was celebrating as if there had never been a crash in 2008.

But on the 80th anniversary of the 1929 crash, October 18, the Bible of Capitalism, the *Wall Street Journal*, raised the same haunting question as the Bible Code:

"Is this the 1930s all over again?"

Why? Unemployment was still at record levels, near 10 percent. The housing crisis that triggered the crash was "getting even worse." And worst of all, the U.S. Government deficit was $1.4 trillion, the biggest since 1945.

"The last time the economy tried to climb out of a deep slump while already this deeply in debt was . . . the 1930s," warned the Journal.

And again it raised the haunting question: "Are we deep into a replay of the Great Depression, an era filled with false dawns?"

In fact, the Bible Code warned we might be.

"Depression USA" was encoded with "starting 2008," and also with "in 2012."

○ DEPRESSION USA   △ STARTING 5768 = 2008   ☐ IN 5772 = 2012

"Recession United States" was also encoded parallel to "death in stocks," and between the two the Bible stated "five years."

Professor Rips calculated the odds. He told me that they were more than 2 million to 1 against that grim financial prediction appearing by chance.

I regretted not having told anyone when I found the forecast of "economic crisis" in 2007, but there was no one to tell.

If I had tried to warn the Bush White House, no one would have believed a 5 year recession possible at the height of the boom.

O RECESSION UNITED STATES   O DEATH IN STOCKS   △ FIVE YEARS   □ ECONOMIC

So I just called my broker, and told him to sell everything. "You're crazy," he said, "we're in the biggest bull market in history."

Once more the Bible Code had predicted what no one believed possible,
and again it had already started to come true.

———

It ALL BEGAN suddenly on Monday September 15, 2008. The stock market had
its worst one-day crash since 9/11.

This time it was not a terrorist attack, but the collapse of Lehman Brothers,
one of Wall Street's five biggest investment firms, that triggered the crisis.

It went bankrupt Sunday night, setting off a chain reaction that left none
of the five standing. The *Wall Street Journal* called it "THE WEEKEND THAT
WALL STREET DIED."

O 15th ELUL = 15th SEPTEMBER, 2008   △ THE DEPRESSIONS

▽ THE END OF MONEY   ☐ IN EVERY COUNTRY

Many economists believe September 15, 2008 was the start of the global economic crisis.

The same day in the Biblical calendar, "15 Elul," appears with "the Depressions" in the Bible Code, and is crossed by "in every country." Just below the code matrix states "the end of money."

The detail of the prediction of today's news in a 3000 year old text is extraordinary.

No newspaper, not the *Wall Street Journal* or the *New York Times*, no television network, no one at all reporting the news as it is happening foresaw the overnight fall of a once mighty investment firm, or the series of crises that would follow.

But it was in the code, the news told thousands of years ago.

The exact day. How could it possibly be encoded so perfectly in the Bible?

The code had predicted the 2008 crash a year in advance, it had foretold the date it began and it warned of the economic crisis that followed.

It was all confirmed on December 1, 2008, when it was officially announced that the United States had been in a recession for a full year, since December 1, 2007.

I was horrified to see what had been foretold in the Bible Code unfolding before my eyes.

On that same day I sent the new Treasury Secretary, Timothy Geithner, a letter telling him that the code warned "that we are just beginning a deep recession that would last at least four more years, until 2012, Obama's entire first term."

My letter gave Geithner no false reassurance. I did not claim to have a solution.

"If there is a solution," I wrote, "that may well also be encoded, but this is not a crystal ball—we can only find answers to questions we know to ask. You may know the questions."

Geithner never responded.

Two hours after I sent him my letter, the *Wall Street Journal* reported that "the Dow closed down nearly 680 points amid growing fears of a protracted global economic slowdown."

On February 10, 2009, Geithner unveiled his eagerly awaited plan to stabilize the credit markets and save the banks with $2.5 trillion in government and private money.

Stock prices immediately fell 382 points, the worst sell-off since Inauguration Day. By the end of the week the market was down another 5% in just four days.

No matter how many hundreds of billions, even trillions, of dollars the Federal government pumped into the failing banks, corporations, and mortgage markets, the entire American and world economy just kept spiraling down.

———

IT WAS CLEAR that our economy had to be rebuilt from total ruin.

At the height of his campaign, on September 16, the day after Wall Street died, Obama said, "What we've seen in the last few days, is nothing less than the final verdict on an economic philosophy that has completely failed."

It was the Republican free market philosophy, an excuse for no regulation of Wall Street, an excuse for a tax policy that gave yet more money to the wealthiest fraction of one percent, who already owned more than half the assets of America.

Just two weeks in office, fighting Congress to get more money to jumpstart the economy, Obama said, "By now it's clear to everyone that we have inherited an economic crisis as deep and dire as any since the days of the Great Depression."

Worse yet, no one seemed to know what to do, which industries to save, which to let die, how to get the banks to start lending money to the companies that could no longer meet their payrolls, and were instead slashing hundreds of thousands of jobs.

On Friday, February 13, 2009 Congress finally approved Obama's $787 billion stimulus plan. That, too, was predicted.

"Obama" was encoded with "bailout" and "recession." The code stated that the new President would try to save a gridlocked economy with government spending.

ל ג ל ו ו ג ה ר ג ה ר ת א כ ס י ד ו י ד ב ר י ה ו י א ל מ ש ה ל א מ ר ד ב ד ר ל ב נ י י ש ר א ל א ו מ ר
ה ה ע ד ה פ ה ד ע ה ב ב ר ב ק ר א ת ד ל ע ל ה ל ל ה ל ר י נ ר י ה ו י ח נ ת ה ו ו נ ג ס ו כ מ ש פ
ה ה ה ל כ ס ל ע ש ה ב ה ג ג ה ו ה נ פ ש ו ש א ע ת ש ה ב י ד ר ה מ ה מ ה א ר ח ו מ ה ו ה ו ג ר
מ ח ו ל מ ה ר ל ח נ ה ו י ו ו ר א ב נ ו ס י מ ת נ כ א ש ר ו צ ה י ו ה י א ת מ ש ה ת ו
ה ה ס מ א נ י י ה ו ל א י ל ס כ ו ר ה ק נ ת ח ה ו י כ ל ע ד ת נ ו ה ב נ ו ' ש ע ב נ ו ל י ו ד ת ו ו נ א ב
ש ו ק נ ה ו ל כ ס מ ה ת נ ה ק ר ת ה ו ה ר ו כ ל ע ד ת נ ו ו ה ת נ ש א ו ש י מ ו ל ע י ה ל י ה ו ק נ ט ר
ר א ל ב א ר ו מ א ר ל א נ ל ה ה מ ה ל ל כ ה מ ע ט ס כ ח י ה ו נ ז ת א מ ר ו צ ת נ ב ת ל ר ד ו ש ל
ר ת א ס מ ת ת ה ו ר נ א ן ו ה מ ש ש א נ ר ה ת א ה ו נ ו ו י ק פ ה נ ר ו ן נ י ה ו ו י ו ג נ י ה ל א ע י ל
ד מ ת ח נ ה ת ת ה נ י ו ה ב ל א ל נ ת כ א ל ש ו ל ה ס ד ו י י ו נ ה י ד ו ו י י ה ו ע ד ה ו נ י ר י ב
ב ר י ה ו ה י א ל א ל ש מ א ר ו מ א נ ת כ א ל ש ו י י י ל ה כ ה ז נ ל ה נ ו ' ' ד ו ה י ה ' ' ר נ ח ת ח ת ה ה ת מ
ש ה ה ל ל י ' ' י ל ל כ ב ד ע ל י ' ' ' נ ב ה ת ד ע י ' ש ' ר א ש ל מ ה ת ר נ ת נ ל ע ל ה ו ש י ל א נ ו מ א ל כ ה ת א

O BAILOUT   △ RECESSION   ▽ OBAMA

At the end of February, 2009 Obama delivered a radical $3.6 trillion budget to Congress, trying to wipe away 30 years of Ronald Reagan's conservative economics, and return America to the New Deal of Franklin Roosevelt.

The next day the stock market hit a new 12 year low, just above 7000, half its peak in 2007, when the code predicted the crisis.

Remaking America, returning it to economic justice and sanity, was not going to be easy.

———

"WHAT'S GOOD FOR General Motors is good for the country," its president had famously said in the 1950's. Now it was a penny stock owned by the American people.

On June 1, 2009 General Motors, the ultimate corporate icon of America, went bankrupt. GM, the hundred year old company, the world's biggest auto maker, was almost $100 billion in debt, and to save the entire industry the government had to buy 60 percent of GM for $50 billion in taxpayer dollars.

In other words, nationalization.

"Nationalization of GM" was encoded in the Bible, with "debt in a financial crisis," and the year, 2009.

ב ו ר ח ס כ י י ו ח א י ת ק י ר ה ו ס י ו ג ב ה ו ז א ס כ ת א
ח ף ס י ו ו ת א ש י ד ק מ ה ה ד ש ה ת א ל א ג י ל א נ ס א
ס י ר ש ע ו ב מ ה ת מ ש ו פ ס מ ב ס ה ת ב א ת י ב ל ס ה ת ח פ ש
ב ו א ר ה נ ח מ ל ג ד ו ו ע ס י ה נ ש א ר ס ת א ב צ ל ת ו א
ו מ ב ר כ ז ל כ ס ה ח פ ש מ ל ס ה ב ה ת י ב ל י ו ל י י נ ב
י ו ל י י נ ב ד ו ת מ ת ה ק י י נ ב ש א ר ת א נ ש נ ר מ א ל ו
י ו ו ה כ ה ו ר ה א ו ב ר מ ת י א ד י ב ד ע ו מ ל ה א ב ב ס
ש א ל ס א ה ש א ה ל א ו מ א ו ו ה כ ה ה ה ת א ע י ב ש ה ו ס
ק י ו ה י י נ פ ל ה פ ו ו נ מ ו ה כ ה ס ת ו א ף י נ ה ו ו ר
ו ש ע ת ח א ף כ ה ה נ מ ל ו מ ש ב ה ל ו ל ב ת ל ס ס י א ל
ל ו ל ב ת ל ס ס י א ל מ ס ה י ו ש ש ד ק ה ל ק ש ב ל ק ש ס
ל ל א ר ש י י נ ב ד ו ת מ ו י י נ ב ל ו ו ר ה א ל ס י י נ ת נ
ה י י פ ל ע ו נ נ ח י י ו ה י י פ ל ע ו ע נ י ו ת ל ע ה ב
ג י ו כ ב י ו ו ב ש י ו ה ו א ת ו ו א ת ה ו ב ר ק ב ו ש א ף
ו י ב ו נ ד ו ע ו ש ב ה ה נ ח מ ה ת ו ב י ב ס ח ו ש מ ס ה
א ו ש י י נ ב ס מ ו מ ו ת ר כ ו ש א ל ו כ ש א ה ת ו ד א ל ע
ו ס ת ב א ל י ת ע ב ש נ ו ר ש א צ ר א ה ת א ו א ר י ס א י ל

O NATIONALIZATION OF GM   △ DEBT IN A FINANCIAL CRISIS   ◇ 5769=2009

    The unimaginable had happened. And it was not the first shock. The entire financial system had already collapsed, forcing Obama to save capitalism by taking it over.

    The White House immediately quashed rumors that the banks also would soon be nationalized. But the Bible Code predicted that the banks would in fact be nationalized, and quickly.

    "Banks" crossed "nationalization."

    No one called it "nationalization," but, as predicted, in the first week of May 2009 "stress tests" showed that more than half of the biggest banks in the country might not survive without tens of billions more in cash reserves.

    Three of the top banks could not raise the money, and one, the world's biggest, Citigroup, sold one-third of its stock to the Federal government.

    In other words, nationalization.

```
א ע ס ש ו ו ן ש ד ה ה ס ו ק מ ל א ה מ ד ק ח ב ז מ ה ל צ א ה
ח ח י נ ח י ו ה ש א א ו ה ה ל ע ש א ה ל ע ר ש א ס י צ ע
ו ה נ ב ל ה י ל ע ן ת נ ו ו ן מ ש ה י ל ע ק צ י ו ו נ ב ר
א ו ה כ ה ר י ט ק ה ו ה ת נ ⓑ ל ל כ ל ע ה נ מ ש מ ו ה ת
י ש א מ ס י ש ד ק ש ד ק ו י Ⓘ ב ל ו ו ר ה א ל ה ח נ מ ה
ו מ ש ב ס י ח ש מ ת ו צ מ י Ⓟ י ק ר ו ו מ ש ב ת ל ל ו ב
ה ח נ מ ו מ ש ה י ל ע ת ק צ Ⓘ ו ס י ת פ ה ת א ת ו ת פ ה
ב י ו ק ה ו ־ ו ה י ל │ה│ש│א│מ│ה│ ש ע י ו ש א ה ח נ מ ה ת
ח י נ ח י ו ה ש א ה ח ב ז מ ה ר י ט ק ה ו ה ת ה ר כ ז א ת
י ל ו ב י ר ק ת ר ש א ה ח נ מ ה ל כ ־ ו ה י י ש א מ ס י
י ל ס ת א ו ב י ר ק ת ת י ש א ר ו ן ב ר ק ־ ו ה י ל ה ש א
```

○ BANKS ☐ NATIONALIZATION

It radically changed the American economy, a government takeover of General Motors and Citigroup, two of the biggest corporations in the country. The taxpayers already owned the world's biggest insurance company AIG, and the two biggest mortgage lenders—in fact, they were propping up the entire financial system.

America, Inc. It was a "last resort" that like everything else was happening so fast the code predictions became reality while I was still writing this book.

Only by running the U.S. Treasury's printing press overtime, creating new money with nothing to back it except more debt, was America able to keep the economy from collapsing entirely.

And fear had turned into outrage. Why had no one been punished, why was taxpayer money in fact being used to pay billion dollar bonuses to the very corporate executives who had brought down the economy?

———

WITH NO COP on the beat, Wall Street created worthless paper, what the *Washington Post* later called "a frenzied, foolhardy drive for upfront fees that brought down the world's financial markets and triggered the largest Federal bailout in history."

When a man everyone considered a brilliant investor, a pillar of the financial community, Bernard Madoff, was discovered to instead be a brazen swindler who stole $60 billion in a Ponzi scheme, he came to embody the criminal lunacy.

He, too, was encoded in the Bible.

O MADOFF   △ SWINDLER   □ HE STUCK OUT

"Madoff" appeared with "swindler" and "he stuck out." That was really the entire point of the scandal. Madoff stuck out—but how different was his crime from the never prosecuted crimes of the investment industry as a whole?

Finally, a year after the bailout, the biggest surviving investment bank, Goldman Sachs, was sued for fraud by the government. The SEC said Goldman had created mortgage securities designed to fail, sold billions to its customers, and at the same time bet against them.

It was not just a hedge. Goldman picked the worst mortgages, the ones certain to go bust, labeled them AAA, sold them as a solid investment, and made billions betting they would fail.

"Goldman Sachs" was encoded in the Bible with "swindlers" and "financial crisis."

O GOLDMAN   ⬠ SACHS   ◇ SWINDLERS   ☐ FINANCIAL   ▽ CRISIS

Unlike Madoff, Goldman had actually helped bring down the world economy. Worse yet, many of Obama's top financial advisors had come from Goldman Sachs.

To many in America it looked like they had bailed out their pals on Wall Street and left the rest of the country to pay the bill.

————

All over America, indeed all over the world, people were losing their homes, their jobs and their pensions. Nearly 15 million people were now unemployed in the United States. Everywhere in the world employment was at its lowest level since World War II.

The same thing was happening all across Europe, and Standard & Poor's declared that Great Britain was in danger of losing its AAA credit rating. The entire country.

The economic crisis was global.

O GLOBAL RECESSION △ 5772 = 2012 ▽ RECESSION

"Global Recession" was encoded with "2012." Again, 2012 appeared to be less the end of the crisis than its peak.

Even Roosevelt had not been able to turn around the economy in his first term, and it appeared that Obama also might not.

The real question seemed to be if 2012 would end the crisis — or be the year the world economy finally fell over a cliff.

Somewhere in the Bible Code perhaps there was a solution.

At first, the only good news I could find came from Professor Rips, who quoted an ancient commentary on the Bible that said God, in his mercy, turned Joseph's predicted "seven years of famine" into only two.

But I was looking for an answer short of Divine intervention. Finally, I found it in the Bible Code.

O YEAR 5770 = 2010 = HE CHANGED 2010   △ OBAMA   ☐ FINANCIAL   ▽ CODES

A code matrix suggested the economy might turn around in 2010 — itself a miracle, but of our making.

"Obama" crossed "year 2010," and "financial" appeared in the same place, with "codes."

In Hebrew "year 2010" also spelled "he changed 2010."

Federal Reserve Chairman Bernanke, echoing the Bible Code, said that the recession would continue through all of 2009, but that 2010 might be a "year of recovery."

In his first address to Congress, President Obama offered hope:

"While our economy may be weakened and our confidence shaken, though we are living in difficult and uncertain times, I want every American to know this—We will rebuild, we will recover, and the United States will emerge stronger than before."

There were doomsayers. Nobel laureate economist Paul Krugman wrote in the *New York Times*, "Things are still getting worse."

"The most you can say is that things are getting worse more slowly," said Krugman. "Even in the Great Depression things didn't head straight down."

He was worried: "This looks an awful lot like the beginning of a second Great Depression. So this is our moment of truth. Will we in fact do what's necessary to prevent Great Depression II?"

What worried me most was not the economy, but the horror that might follow its collapse, not Great Depression II, but World War III.

It was a global economic crisis that triggered World War II, and another global depression could create total chaos in an already dangerous world, and set off a third World War.

Or a nuclear terror attack could create an economic crisis, indeed send the world back to the barter system. And even Warren Buffett, the ultimate investor, said, "Nuclear terror is, unfortunately, inevitable."

So, of course, I wanted to believe everything would be resolved in 2010. The code only tells us the odds, not the final outcome. We will decide our own fate.

As we headed into the Spring in March 2010, the *Wall Street Journal* celebrated a remarkable year-long rally, the Dow up more than 60% from its frightening low in March 2009.

"AMERICA'S BACK!" Newsweek proclaimed in a cover story in April 2010.

But unemployment was still near 10%, one in four homes were "underwater," the mortgages now greater than the value of the real estate, and America's deficit was so out of control it was estimated that the national debt would be 90% of the economy by 2020.

In Europe things were even worse. Greece was bankrupt, its debt declared "junk bonds." Spain and Portugal had been downgraded, and it looked like Italy was next. The entire Euro Zone might crash, and the British debt was second only to Greece.

But the Dow had passed 11,000, and everybody on Wall Street was partying like it was . . . the Roaring 20's.

Then, on Thursday May 6, 2010, the Dow suddenly dropped almost 1000 points in five minutes, a flashback to the panicked selling of 2008. Although the freefall lasted only minutes, it exposed a fault line in the markets, and left them shaken.

Was the party over?

Can Obama really turn around the American economy, and with it the world economy, prevent a depression and a war, in just two years, in 2010? It remains a question.

In fact, in Hebrew, the year 2010 is written in letters that also spell a question—"Will you save?"

CHAPTER FOUR

HEADLINE NEWS

EVENTS THAT JUST yesterday made headlines are consistently encoded in the Bible, in a text that is 3000 years old.

In fact, the recent past appears in such accurate detail that the predicted future seems like tomorrow's headlines.

The news reported in the Bible Code thousands of years ago is the same as the news reported in the *New York Times*, *Washington Post*, or *Wall Street Journal* the day it happens.

And it is not only as accurate, it is sometimes more accurate.

On September 11, 2001, right after the Twin Towers fell, Professor Rips discovered an extraordinary code matrix.

○ SEPTEMBER 11, 2001 (23 ELUL) ◌ TWIN ◇ TOWERS

□ AND THERE DIED OF THE PEOPLE THAT DAY ABOUT 3000 MEN

"Twin Towers" crossed the Biblical date equivalent to 9/11. In the same place the original words of the Bible said, "And there died of the people that day about 3000 men".

Rips called me the day of the attack. "The code states 3000, but it must be wrong," he said, "because all the news reports say 6000."

It was not until months later that it was determined that the real number of dead was just under 3000.

But the Bible Code stated the true death toll on the day of the attack.

By the time we knew that, the United States was planning a war against Saddam Hussein, an invasion of Iraq.

O DEATH. WHO IS DESTROYED? HUSSEIN   □ 5763 (2003)

◇ IT WAS CONFIRMED, HE FLED

I was summoned to Washington to meet with the entire top command of American military intelligence at the Pentagon.

On February 21, 2003, the Admirals and Generals plotting the invasion sat down with me for an hour to find out the future foretold in the Bible Code.

"What does it say about Iraq?" asked Lin Wells, the director of C3I, military shorthand for Command, Control, Communications, and Intelligence.

"Good news," I said handing him a code matrix. "Saddam Hussein will fall in 2003."

"So the outcome is already determined?" asked a General from the Joint Chiefs of Staff.

"No," I said. "The Bible Code is not a crystal ball. It reveals probabilities, nothing is set in stone."

But on December 14, 2003 Saddam Hussein was in fact captured, hiding in a hole in the ground, after a member of his clan accepted a $50 million bribe from the CIA.

Later he was hanged, "death" just as the code had predicted.

Of course, that did not stop Al Qaeda. Saddam Hussein had not attacked America on 9/11. Iraq was irrelevant to the war on terror. The danger was Osama bin Laden, as I had tried to tell all the intelligence officials at the Pentagon.

○ TRAINS SABOTAGED △ SPAIN ☐ IT WILL KILL THE PEOPLE

On March 11, 2004 Al Qaeda blew up four passenger trains in Madrid, killing 191 people, and injuring more than 1,700.

It was revenge for Spain's participation in the war in Iraq. But it was Al Qaeda that attacked. Indeed, Bin Laden had warned, "All who cooperate with the Americans against Iraq are hostile to Islam."

○ SIVAN 5765 = JULY 2005   △ SUBWAY   ▽ TRAIN   ◇ BOMBS
□ BECAUSE YOU WENT TO WAR

On July 7, 2005 Al Qaeda struck again against an American ally, England. A homegrown terror cell trained in Pakistan bombed the London subway, killing 52 people, and wounding more than 700.

Again it was encoded in the Bible. "Subway" "train" and "bombs" all appeared with July 2005. In a second matrix "subway" was crossed by "terror" and "London."

"Because you went to war" appeared in the original words of the Bible right below July 2005.

Al Qaeda blamed the attack on British Prime Minister Tony Blair, who sent troops to Iraq.

The words of the Bible — "because you went to war" - echoed Bin Laden's deputy Al-Zawahiri: "Blair has brought you destruction in central London, and he will bring more of that, God willing."

On November 26, 2008, in the most brazen terrorist attack since 9/11, Islamic militants from Pakistan closely tied to Al Qaeda laid siege for three days to India's commercial center, Mumbai.

Seventy gunmen armed with machine guns and hand grenades, acting with military precision, attacked two luxury hotels, the main train station, and a hospital, killing 172 people.

Many suspected Pakistani intelligence was involved, that 70 militants could not have on their own taken over a major city.

The terror attack brought two nuclear armed nations, India and Pakistan, to the brink of war. It showed how militants, even without a nuclear weapon, might trigger a nuclear holocaust.

It was all encoded in the Bible in amazing detail.

On the third day of the attack as a final act the terrorists executed five hostages at a Jewish center, Chabad House, in Mumbai, the city called Bombay when the British ruled India.

"Terror" "in Bombay" appeared with "in Chabad House."

Professor Rips showed me something extraordinary in the matrix.

During the attack on the Jewish center a Torah scroll was hit by gunfire, ripping out part of two verses of the Bible. It was in exactly that place that "Terror" "Bombay" and "in Chabad House" appeared in the code.

BOMBAY ○ TERROR ○ IN CHABAD HOUSE

BOMBAY ○ TERROR ○ IN CHABAD HOUSE

A month later, on December 27, 2008, Pakistani militants tied to Al Qaeda again struck, assassinating Benazir Bhutto.

The former Prime Minister had returned to bring democracy back to Pakistan after years of military rule.

"Bhutto Assassination" was encoded in the Bible with her first name "Benazir," and "target."

O BHUTTO ASSASSINATION   □ TARGET   ▽ BENAZIR

She was seen as a friend to the West, and a threat to both Al Qaeda and the military junta that ruled Pakistan.

The CIA concluded that Al Qaeda had conspired with other Islamic militants to kill her, but again many believed that Pakistan's own intelligence agency had conspired with the assassins.

The murder took place in a garrison city under tight military control, in fact, Pakistan's Army Headquarters, where the even more powerful Inter-Services Intelligence agency (ISI) actually ruled. ISI had helped to create Al Qaeda and the other militant groups that it now accused of killing Bhutto.

Like the attack on India a month earlier, it raised a question of whether there was any real difference between the rulers of Pakistan and the terrorists it gave a safe haven.

In any event, Bhutto's assassination plunged the world's most unstable nuclear-armed nation into ever deeper crisis.

———

NATURE CAN BE as dangerous as terrorism.

Only a major natural disaster can threaten the world as much as a nuclear attack, and major natural disasters are also encoded in the Bible exactly as they appeared in newspaper headlines.

On December 27, 2004 the *New York Times* reported that "the world's most powerful earthquake in 40 years erupted underwater off the Indonesian island of Sumatra, and sent walls of water barreling thousands of miles across South East Asia."

Everyone called it "the Asian Tsunami" and the final death toll reached 178,000, with 50,000 missing and presumed dead.

"Asia" crossed "Tsunami" in the code one time, and right above the original words of the Bible told of a "wall of water to the right and to the left."

○ ASIA   ◻ TSUNAMI   ☐ WALL OF WATER TO THE RIGHT AND TO THE LEFT   ○ WALL OF WATER

"Wall of water" appeared a second time, using exactly the same words as the Times report of the 40 foot high waves traveling at speeds up to 500 miles an hour that crashed into India, Sri Lanka, Thailand, and Malaysia, as well as Indonesia.

"Wall of water" came from a famous passage in the Bible that told the story of Moses parting the Red Sea, allowing the ancient Israelites to walk through on dry land, then drowning the pursuing Egyptians.

Remarkably, in exactly the same place in the Bible, Exodus 14, the words "Asia" and "Tsunami" cross each other uniquely in the 3000 year old text.

On August 29, 2005 Hurricane Katrina hit New Orleans, and the next day two levees broke, flooding the city, killing more than 1,300 people. That, too, was encoded in the Bible.

"In New" "Orleans" appeared with "storm" crossed by "death."

O IN NEW   O ORLEANS   △ STORM   □ DEATH

Again, the same report that was in the Times, on CNN, that made head-lines everywhere in the world was also encoded and foreseen in the Bible.

It was the worst natural disaster in America in 100 years, and it raised a frightening question for the country.

If our government could not save the people of New Orleans from a hur-ricane it knew was coming 3 days in advance, how could it deal with a far greater disaster, that would come with no warning, like a nuclear terror attack?

Katrina, and the bodies floating in New Orleans, became the image that as much as Iraq brought down President Bush.

On January 12, 2010 a massive earthquake struck Haiti, killing at least 200,000. The epicenter was the island country's capital, Port-au-Prince, a city of more than two million in the poorest nation of the Western hemisphere.

○ HAITI DESTROYED IN ONE BLOW   △ EARTHQUAKE   □ DEATH OF A PEOPLE

"Haiti destroyed in one blow" is encoded with "earthquake," and "death of a people" appears in the same matrix.

It was as if the code was reporting the death of a country.

It had been hit by two major hurricanes in 2008, and now by the worst earthquake in more than 200 years, as the Times reported, "bringing even more suffering to a nation that was already the poorest and most disaster-prone."

Again, the Bible Code echoed the *New York Times* headline, "Fierce Quake Devastates Haitian Capital."

O HAITI △ 5770 (2010) IT OVERWHELMED / THEY DIED ◇ JOB

"Haiti" is also encoded with "2010 it overwhelmed," overlapped by "they died."

The full code captured the endless series of afflictions in Biblical terms—"Job" is encoded just below Haiti, comparing the country to the most plagued character in the Old Testament.

Nature again showed its awful power on March 20, 2010 when a volcano erupted in Iceland, shooting so much ash into the sky that it covered the North Atlantic Ocean and most of Europe.

All air traffic to and from Europe came to a sudden halt. For 5 days, and again weeks later, the modern technological world was paralyzed by a volcano on a tiny distant island.

O IN ICELAND   △ VOLCANO   □ ASH

"In Iceland" was encoded with "volcano" and "ash" in the Bible. Time after time the code foretold what the media reported.

On April 20, 2010 a giant oil rig, for the world's deepest oil well, exploded in the Gulf of Mexico.

O OIL SPILL   △ 5770 = 2010   ◇ EXPLOSION   □ OF FIRE   O AT SEA

"Oil spill" was encoded with "explosion" "of fire" "at sea." The year it happened, 2010 crossed "oil spill."

It was the worst man-made ecological disaster in the history of the United States. Congressional hearings later proved that BP, British Petroleum, had caused the disaster by taking risks to increase profits, and had no plan to deal with the 2.5 million gallons of oil gushing into the gulf every day.

No one knew when the well could be plugged, how much oil would pollute the coastline from Texas to Florida, and then up the Eastern shore, but every 4 days it was spewing out an amount equal to America's biggest prior oil spill.

And no one could explain why BP had been allowed to drill a well a mile under water, without first proving it could do it safely.

"Climate Change" may be the greatest long-term threat we face.

○ CLIMATE CHANGE   □ DAY AND NIGHT, SEVEN DAYS   ◇ TODAY

◌ HEAT WAVE   ⬠ FLOOD

It is encoded with "today" crossing "day and night, seven days."

The message is clear—it is happening right now, 24/7. The long-term impact is also encoded in the same matrix, a "heat wave" that can cause a "flood," indeed a Flood on a Biblical scale. This is exactly the consensus view of scientists, that global warming caused by man-made carbon emissions from all factories, cars, homes, all fossil fuels, will eventually cause the polar icecaps to melt, creating a world-wide flood that will leave all coastal areas underwater.

Former Vice President Al Gore, the man who more than anyone else made the danger of climate change known to the world, and won a Nobel Prize for doing it, was also encoded.

O   NOBEL GORE   □   FROM CODE

O   WE WILL UNDERSTAND

The matrix states that "from the code" "we will understand" "Nobel Gore."

Global Warming is known to be a man-made natural disaster. We can prevent it, because we are causing it. What is less well known is that the flood in New Orleans was also a man-made natural disaster, because the levees were poorly built. The oil spill in the Gulf of Mexico is, of course, man-made. And even the Asian tsunami, while it could not have been stopped, would not have killed nearly so many people if an effective warning system had been created.

Indeed, the disaster we must fear most would be entirely man-made. Nuclear terror, which can kill millions, annihilate great cities, even destroy human civilization, can also be prevented.

And we do not need to worry about the impact of Global Warming a hundred years from now, if we don't prevent nuclear terror right now.

———

IN JANUARY 2009 Barack Obama replaced George Bush, and America finally shifted its focus from Iraq to Al Qaeda.

But Osama bin Laden had long since disappeared. The leader of Al Qaeda, the mastermind behind every terrorist attack, had not been seen or heard since December 2001.

Eight years after Bin Laden disappeared, on December 1, 2009, President Obama in a nationally televised speech, announced that he was sending 30,000 more troops into Afghanistan, to fight Al Qaeda. That headline, too, was encoded.

O AFGHAN   △ WAR   □ DANGER, BE CAREFUL

The Bible Code appeared to state Obama was taking a risk. "Afghan" "war" was encoded with "danger, be careful."

I worried that it was an unnecessary risk, that Obama might be fighting the wrong war.

Many, even in Obama's own party, were saying it—that the eight year war in Afghanistan served no purpose, and had not since Bin Laden was allowed to escape to Pakistan.

Bin Laden was thought still to be in Pakistan, a country that also had 100 nuclear weapons mounted on missiles. And our military commander, General David Petraeus, told Congress there were few, if any, Al Qaeda fighters in Afghanistan.

Did Al Qaeda need an Afghan base? The 9/11 attack was conceived in Malaysia and plotted by an Al Qaeda cell in Hamburg, Germany.

They then learned to fly, and hijacked jets in America. The 19 men who carried out the attack came from Egypt and Saudi Arabia.

Bin Laden only blessed the plan in Afghanistan. He could have done it from Pakistan, or indeed, from any place in the world.

Obama correctly named our true enemy, Al Qaeda, in a speech at West Point. But although he also correctly stated the threat was "nuclear terror," just as the Bible Code warned, he did not say how 100,000 U.S. troops in Afghanistan could protect New York or Washington from a nuclear attack.

Later, it was revealed that before Obama sent more troops into Afghanistan, both the President's National Security Advisor and his Counter-Terror Advisor had met with the heads of Pakistan's military, and delivered a blunt message—fight Al Qaeda, or the United States would itself carry the battle into Pakistan.

"Negotiations will not lead Al Qaeda leaders to lay down their arms," said the President.

Obama, after all, did seem to be focused on the real danger—Al Qaeda and nuclear terror.

But tomorrow's headline could still be the danger stated in the Bible Code, because the code reveals that Al Qaeda might already have nuclear weapons.

And no one in American intelligence is dealing with the danger.

CHAPTER FIVE

DENIAL

ON CHRISTMAS DAY, December 25, 2009, a young Nigerian trained by Al Qaeda in Yemen boarded an airplane in Amsterdam headed for Detroit. He had enough explosives hidden in his underwear to bring the plane down.

It should have been the beginning of a great awakening in U.S. intelligence.

Incredibly, everything needed to stop the terrorist was known before Abdul Mutallab boarded the plane, and yet no one stopped him. It was known that a Nigerian was training with Al Qaeda in Yemen to attack the United States. His father had warned the U.S. Embassy and the CIA in Nigeria that Mutallab had become a dangerous militant. It was even known the attack was planned for Christmas, and yet nothing was done to prevent it.

An enraged President Obama called it a "systemic failure" of American intelligence. But Obama did not know that the very man he appointed to investigate it, his counter-terror advisor John Brennan, was at that very moment ignoring a new warning from Yemen—of nuclear terror.

Over New Year's weekend I called Brennan at his home, and told him that Israeli intelligence had confirmed an Al Qaeda base in Yemen where Osama bin Laden might already have nuclear weapons.

I did not immediately mention the Bible Code, but in the 3000 year old code was all the information about the failed Christmas bombing, and the far greater danger from Yemen, nuclear terror.

"Christmas time" was encoded with the name of the 23 year old Nigerian terrorist, "Mutallab." Right below his name he was precisely identified, "suicide bomber, young man."

נ ת ת ה ע ל כ ת פ נ ו ת ת פ א ת ד א ל מ ל ו י ל פ נ י נ ו י י ע ש י ת ש ת י ט ב ע ו ת ז ה ה
ה ש ב ע ת י מ י ת ע י מ ס ה מ לֹ א י ד ו ס י פ ו ר ו ח א ת ת ע ש ה ל י וֹ ת ש ע ל ה כ ב ר י ׳ םֹ
ש ב ת מ י ת מ י ת נ ו מ י ת ה נ י ב נ י י ׳ ש ר א ל א ת ה ה ש ב ת ל ע ש י ו ת א נ ת ה ה ש ב
ל ת א ס ו נ א מ צ ת א נ ח י נ ב ע י ׳ נ י ׳ ה ד י ו ת נ נ א ת ת ד ד ד ו כ ז ו נ א ךֹ ד ר עֹ ל
ו ת א כ ל ׳ ה ר י ה ה נ א ת נ ר י ה א ת ש מ ן א נ ת מ ז א ב ת ח ה ה ק ט ו ר ט ע ת ר ו ת ו
ע ש נ א ה ה פ ה כ ר ת כ ל ר ת ו ג מ י ל ת י ו ו ש ט נ ג ו י ש ש ו ט מ ז ו ר ה מ ע ש ה
ו מ נ מ ס י ו ׳ ה י ׳ מ נ ת כ ר ה ל צ ר ס כ ה ר ה ת נ א ד נ ג י ׳ ה ק ד ק ש י ו נ א תֹ א נֹ א ד
ם ם שֹ נ ח ת ס פֹ כ ב נ יֹ ל ס י ׳ ל ו י ר ׳ לֹ ו ר ת ו ה ס ו י ׳ ע ע ש ש מ שֹ כ כ ל אֹ ו ר צ ו ה י ׳ ה י ׳ ו
ת נ ת ר נ ת ל ע ב כ ד ב ע ל ה כ ל ׳ ס ׳ י י ׳ נ ה ה ק ט ו ׳ ו ר א נ ת ז י ׳ ס פ לֹ טֹ נ א
א ת נ א ר ת ו כ ה ה נ ת ה י ׳ י ר ת ד ה ו בֹ כ ש ב ה ה נ ש יֹ ו ש ע י ׳ ט ז י ׳ ת נ ף ס םֹ ל ט אֹ כ
א ת ד סֹ ה ש ל מ י ׳ ה ר ב ת נ ח ב ת ר ש ב ה י ׳ ה י ׳ ׳ י ׳ ו נ ת ד שֹ ל מ י ׳ ב י ׳ ׳ ו ס י ם ק ב ז
ל א נ ב ש ו פ ה נ ה מ ד ו י ו ל ש ב כ א ן נ ו ב ו א ל נ כ ׳ ׳ ו אֹ נ ה ל ה ס מ א ש ל
ו פ ס ת ל כ א ו ׳ ׳ ט ט מ א נ ה כ ל א נ כ ר ב כ ל ת ב כ נ א ת ר ׳ ת י ל ע מ ת ׳ ל תֹ נ ג כ
ח ו ר ת ל ל ה א ל ו ש ב ע ת ׳ ׳ מ י ה ס ב ט י ׳ ה ג ׳ ׳ ל נ ג ל ה ת א כ נ ל ב ש י ׳ ו כ ׳ ל שֹ ו
ו ה י ׳ ז ב ת ו מ כ א נ ל ג ׳ ׳ ע י ב נ ג י כ ל ל ב ר א ש ׳ ו ר ׳ ׳ ׳ ה ת ת נ י ט מ ע א ד הֹ ע ו ר
ש ה ר ש ב ׳ ׳ ע י ב ׳ ׳ ׳ ׳ ש ל ו ׳ ה נ כ ת ש פ נ ת א נ ׳ו ׳ ׳ ׳ י ׳ ׳ נ כ ס ו י ׳ ל מ כ ס כ ה ל נ א
א ׳ י ׳ ׳ ב ע מ ׳ ׳ י ׳ ׳ ל ׳ ׳ ל א נ ש ׳ ל ׳ ר ל ת נֹ ׳ ׳ נ ל ׳ ל ׳ נ ל ל ׳ ה א ׳ נ ס מ א כ ך ׳ ד ׳
א ׳ ר ח י ׳ ׳ ל ׳ ׳ ס ׳ כ ל א א ׳ ת ׳ ׳ נ אֹ ׳ ר ל ׳ ׳ ת ׳ נ א ס ׳ ׳ כ ׳ ׳ ל א ו ס ׳ י ר ל ח נ י ׳ א
ו מ ש ב ה ה נ ל ו ל ב ת ל שֹׁ ס ׳ ׳ נ ר ש ע נ ׳ ׳ ש ׳ הֹ נ ׳ מ ׳ ׳ ׳ נ ׳ ל ל ׳ ה ל ל ע ׳ ו ו ו ׳
ז ת א ׳ ל ד מ ר ד ו ׳ ע נ ו ׳ י ז ת א כ ל ד ד ש ׳ ׳ ׳ ה י ׳ ׳לֹ ת ב ש צ ׳ ל א ה ׳ ׳ ה ׳ ׳ ׳ י ׳ ׳ נ ת ב ש ו
כ ה ׳ו ׳ נ ת ב ׳ ׳ נ כ ש מ ׳ ׳ ת ת נ ׳ ׳ א ׳ ׳ צ ׳ ׳ ו ת ש ׳דֹ ׳ ׳ ׳ נ פ מֹ ׳ ׳ ו ׳ ׳ י ׳ ׳ ׳ ׳ ו ׳ ׳ ׳
ש א ו נ ת נ ׳ ק מ נ ה ׳ ד ש נ ת א ס א ׳ ׳ ׳ נ ת ׳ ת נ א ׳ ה ה ׳ ׳ נ ת ת ׳ נ ׳ ׳ סֹ ה ׳ ה נ נ ׳ ׳ ת ׳ ׳ ׳
ש מ ת א ׳ * ׳ ו ׳ ה ׳ ׳ ה ׳ ו ׳ צ ר ו ש א נ ל ׳ כ כ ל ׳ כ ל א ר ש ׳ ׳ ׳ ׳ נ ׳ ב ׳ ו ׳ ש עֹ ׳ ו נ ׳ ׳ נ ׳ ׳ ׳ ד ע ה ׳ נ ׳ ם מ
ל ע ׳לֹ ׳ ׳ ח ׳ ׳ ב א ׳ נ ׳ ב ל א ׳ ׳ ׳ ׳ ׳ צ ׳ ׳ ׳ ׳ ׳ ר ׳ ׳ ר ד ד מ ת ת ה פ ש מ ב ל ב א תֹ ׳ ׳ ב א ׳ ׳ ש ׳ ׳ ו ׳ ם ׳
ש מ ׳ ד י ׳ ו ק פ פ ה ל א ס ׳ ׳ו ׳ ש ׳ ל ש ׳ ו ׳ ת נ ו א מ ש ׳ ו ׳ ו ס ׳ ׳ פ ל א םֹ נ ב א נ ת ׳ ׳ ב ׳ ל ה ת ס ם ׳
כ ה ה ׳ ש ׳ ע ו ׳ ת נ ׳ ׳ ו צ מ מ ס ׳ ל ל ס ׳ ׳ ל ׳ ע * ׳ ה ׳ ׳ ו ׳ ל ׳ ׳ ׳ ס ׳ ׳ י ׳ מ ל ש ח ת ב ז ׳ ה ש ׳ ע ׳ ׳ ל ׳ ׳ א ת ת נ א ׳ ׳
׳ ב ׳ דֹ ׳ נ א נ ש ב ׳ כ ׳ ד ת ׳ נ א ׳ ׳ ל ׳ י ׳ א ׳ ר ׳ ק ׳ ב ׳ ׳ נ ׳ ׳ ב ר ׳ ׳ ת ׳ ר ׳ א ׳ ׳ פ ׳ נ ו ׳ ׳ ע ו פ ׳ ה ׳ ׳ ה ׳ ם ו ׳ ׳ ר ה ׳ ש י ׳ ע י

○ CHRISTMAS TIME △ MUTALLAB ◇ SUICIDE BOMBER YOUNG MAN ▢ 5770 / 2009 ☐ FROM YEMEN
▽ AIRPLANE ▽ FLY ☐ DELTA

Even the name of the airline, "Delta," was encoded with "airplane."

The bomb did not explode. Mutallab could not ignite it. But the plane would have gone down as it was about to land in Detroit if the passengers had not stopped him.

And the same code matrix that named Mutallab also stated "from Yemen."

Suddenly, on Christmas, the failed bombing plot focused everyone on Yemen. But Obama's advisor Brennan still ignored the warning of nuclear terror from Yemen.

On Saturday night May 1, 2010, everyone's focus again suddenly changed.

A Pakistani parked an SUV in Times Square, the heart of New York City. In the van was a bomb that could have killed thousands. It was not detected by police or any of the hundreds of surveillance cameras, but a street vendor.

American officials said Faisal Shahzad was sent by the Taliban, a militant Islamic group closely linked to Al Qaeda. But the car bomb did not explode. It was so poorly made many doubted the Taliban had really trained the Pakistani.

"Times" "Square" was encoded with "he ran from car" "and he was captured."

O TIMES   △ SQUARE   □ HE RAN FROM CAR   ◇ AND HE WAS CAPTURED   □ IYAR = MAY

The terrorist was no better at hiding his identity than at making a bomb. He was quickly found through the person he bought the van from on the Internet.

But he nonetheless almost escaped because the "no fly" list that was supposed to be iron-clad since the failed Christmas bombing still did not work. The Pakistani slipped past an FBI stake-out at his home, easily boarded a plane at JFK, and had to be pulled off the flight to Dubai just minutes before take-off.

As New York Mayor Michael Bloomberg said, "Clearly the guy was on the plane and shouldn't have been. We got lucky."

U.S. intelligence claimed that the failed Christmas bombing and the failed Times Square bombing proved that Al Qaeda could no longer stage a large-scale attack like 9/11.

In fact, Obama's counter-terror advisor Brennan, who failed to try to prevent a nuclear terror attack, was quick to claim that the failure of these two terrorist attacks were evidence of the success of American intelligence.

"They now are relegated to trying to do these unsophisticated attacks," Brennan boasted on CNN, "showing that they have inept capabilities and training."

All the expert reports that Al Qaeda was pursuing weapons of mass destruction, that a nuclear terror attack was likely by 2013, were forgotten.

What everyone failed to see was that the two terrorist attacks failed only because the terrorists were incompetent.

What no one mentioned was that the failed Times Square bombing exposed the incompetence of American intelligence just as the failed Christmas bombing had.

"This is the most dangerous time I've seen since 9/11," said the head of the 9/11 Commission Thomas Kean.

"Al Qaeda is constantly learning our weaknesses, and the U.S. intelligence community is dysfunctional."

"If we don't get our act together, we're going to be in serious trouble," Kean said. "We can't count on the terrorists being incompetent forever."

What everyone instead pretended, that Bin Laden would give up his plan for an "American Hiroshima," was just wishful thinking.

In fact, the Bible Code stated that the nuclear terror plot was already in progress.

———

FOR YEARS I had been trying to warn America and Israel that the nuclear weapon would come from Pakistan, but be used by Al Qaeda in Yemen.

However, instead of amateurs, the danger was the mastermind of 9/11, Osama bin Laden, and the scientist who built Pakistan's own weapons, A.Q. Khan.

The code said a dot in the desert of Yemen was, or would soon become, the headquarters for Al Qaeda and the hide-out for the nuclear weapons.

In fact, "Bin Laden" was encoded across "army headquarters" and the exact name of the tiny village where it was located, with detailed information about a place no intelligence agency had ever seen.

I showed that matrix to the deputy director of the CIA, the director of all military intelligence at the Pentagon, and Israel's chief intelligence analyst, all at the same time.

Israeli intelligence, with one satellite, was able to confirm most of what the code stated within weeks. The dot in the desert was an Al Qaeda base and every structure the code named was also photographed by the satellite.

American intelligence, with more satellites than the rest of the world combined, failed to see anything. It could not even find a related site that was on Google Earth.

I also showed the Americans and Israelis a code table that clearly stated "Yemen" as the "sanctuary" for "Al Qaeda," and warned of a "great blow."

O AL QAEDA   □ SANCTUARY YEMEN   □ THE GREAT BLOW

And I showed leaders of the intelligence agencies in both countries a truly chilling statement from the code—the name of the confirmed Al Qaeda base with "atomic" "war."

It could not be more clear. The Bible Code stated that a dot in the remotest desert of Yemen was the headquarters of Al Qaeda and Bin Laden, and the staging area for a nuclear terror attack on Israel and the United States.

It was equally clear in the code that Pakistan, and its nuclear scientist Khan, would be the source of the nuclear weapons.

"Were one to map terrorism and weapons of mass destruction today, all roads would intersect in Pakistan," the 9/11 panel stated, confirming the Bible Code.

O FROM PAKISTAN ☐ IN THE END OF DAYS △ TERRORISM ☐ KHAN

Pakistan is encoded only once in the Bible. And yet "from Pakistan" appears with "terrorism" crossing "in the End of Days." "Khan" is named just below.

"The next terrorist attack against the United States is likely to originate in Pakistan," the 9/11 panel concluded.

What the code states is that the weapon will come from Pakistan, but the attack will come from Al Qaeda in Yemen.

Israel confirmed the location beyond doubt. Every detail stated in the code was photographed by satellite.

———

GENERAL YOSSI KUPERWASSER, Israel's top intelligence analyst, called Obama's top terror advisor Brennan at the White House in January 2010. A week later Brennan sent a CIA officer from the American embassy to see Kuperwasser at his home in Tel Aviv.

Kuperwasser confirmed that the Bible Code had accurately named a remote desert wadi, one dot on the planet, as an Al Qaeda base. He gave the exact coordinates. But he urged Brennan to contact me about the critical missing information, the location of the nuclear weapons.

Israel would continue its search, but Kuperwasser said he was not certain his country could finish the job on its own.

But the Bible Code suggested an "Atomic Weapon" in "Yemen" could be found, perhaps by a more advanced "satellite."

○ ATOMIC WEAPON   △ SATELLITE   ◇ YEMEN

Brennan, however, ignored the Israeli lead.

I called the man who had been Brennan's boss at the CIA, its former Executive Director, Buzzy Krongard, who had already advised Brennan to meet with me. Krongard said, "Tell the Israelis to give John the satellite photos. It's concrete evidence no one can ignore."

In early March I contacted Brennan again. My fax to his White House office stated:

"I just spoke to General Kuperwasser, who told me he has new satellite photographs of the site in Yemen that may be our best lead to nuclear weapons Al Qaeda already has.

"Everything Israel could see by satellite was confirmed, but Israel may lack the resources to find the weapons.

"The danger is not local terrorists in Yemen, but Bin Laden, Al Qaeda central, and the Khan network.

"Our chance to stop them is now. We'll get one chance to do it right. If we fail, we may lose New York and Washington."

Brennan never replied, he never again contacted Kuperwasser, he even refused to look at the satellite photographs.

———

DENIAL IS A stronger instinct than survival.

The self-deception did not begin with John Brennan. It began in the Bush years, before 9/11.

Long before the attack, the CIA knew that 2 of the 19 hijackers, already on a terrorist watch-list, were in the United States, but did not tell the FBI. Only the FBI, however, had the authority to investigate or arrest them inside the country. The FBI had information from its own field offices that its headquarters in Washington ignored—Arabs were taking flight lessons in America that should have raised red flags. They did not want to learn how to take-off or land. They only wanted to learn how to make sharp turns in mid-air.

On September 10, 2001 the National Security Agency, which listens in on the world, picked up two messages in Arabic. They stated, "Tomorrow is the zero hour." But no one translated the intercepts until September 12.

Under normal circumstances the explicit warning would have been ignored for months, because all of American intelligence only had 12 Arabic translators. Only the attack on 9/11 caused NSA to translate the messages that could have stopped the attack the next day.

On the day of the attack the failure was even greater. The most powerful military force in the world was unable to get even one fighter plane in the air, with orders to intercept the four hijacked jets, during the attack on New York and Washington. In fact, it was unable to protect the Pentagon, American military headquarters, almost 2 hours after the first of the Twin Towers was hit. Only the passengers on the fourth hijacked jet fought the terrorists, and prevented the White House from also being destroyed.

O PENTAGON □ DAMAGED ◇ EMERGENCY FROM ARABIA

How could that have happened?

The 9/11 Commission later explained it. No one in American intelligence could believe that people without indoor plumbing could possibly attack the United States, whose mainland had not been attacked in two World Wars.

"An organization like Al Qaeda," stated the Commission, "in a country on the other side of the Earth, in a region so poor that electricity or telephones were scarce, could nonetheless scheme to wield weapons of unprecedented destructive power in the largest cities of the United States.

"The greatest danger of another catastrophic attack in the United States will materialize if the world's most dangerous terrorists acquire the world's most dangerous weapons.

"Al Qaeda has tried to acquire or make nuclear weapons for at least ten years."

However, 10 years after 9/11 we remain totally unprepared for the attack everyone knows is coming. We are looking for the next underpants bomber, or car bomber, not the nuclear bomber.

But the government is not even able to stop the amateurs. On Christmas 2009, as on 9/11, it was the passengers who stopped the terrorists, not any government official. In Times Square on May 1, 2010, it was a street vender.

As the *New York Times* asked in its editorial after the failed Christmas bombing, "WHY DIDN'T THEY SEE IT?" The Times said, "It is incredible, and frightening, that the government cannot do at least as good a job at swiftly updating and correlating information as Google."

The editorial observed that if an intelligence analyst had punched "Nigerian, Mutallab, Yemen" into Google he would have had an answer in seconds. Why couldn't our National Counter-Terrorism Center find the answer at all?

The Bible Code was also able to connect the dots 3000 years ago, and I was able to find all the related information in one code matrix. We did the same thing on 9/11. In fact, the code did it better than any intelligence agency.

Still, no American intelligence agency will look at the codes that predict a nuclear terror attack from Yemen, or even the Israeli satellite photographs that confirm the Al Qaeda base.

Professor Rips foresaw the moment: "The more obvious it becomes the code is real, what it predicts is right, the faster people will run away from you."

———

WE CREATED EVERY monster we face today.

Al Qaeda, and Osama bin Laden, owe their existence to Ronald Reagan's CIA Director, who secretly funded the Arab fighters to help defeat the Soviets in Afghanistan, almost 30 years ago.

The unforeseen result, 9/11.

In December 2001, just three months after 9/11, American troops invading Afghanistan had Bin Laden trapped in his caves in the Tora Bora mountains, at the border with Pakistan. The CIA intercepted his voice in a radio transmission. But Bush left fewer than 100 American troops to block Bin Laden's escape.

"Bin Laden" was, in fact, encoded with "Tora Bora," but also "he slipped away" and "he will carry terror."

○ BIN LADEN □ HE SLIPPED AWAY □ THIS MAN △ TORA △ BORA

◇ HE WILL CARRY TERROR

Bush and Cheney, in their urgency to rush our Special Forces into Iraq, left Afghan warlords to capture the leader of Al Qaeda, the man behind the attacks on New York and Washington.

Instead, they helped Bin Laden escape into Pakistan. He hasn't been seen or heard since.

A year later, as the United States was planning to launch a full-scale invasion of Iraq, I was summoned to Washington to brief the entire top command of American military intelligence at the Pentagon.

When I arrived on February 21, 2003, the White House had just put the country on "high terror alert," Washington was under tight guard, with F-16 fighter jets flying overhead, and armored vehicles mounted with Stinger anti-aircraft missiles patrolling the streets of the nation's capital.

At 9AM all the men who had been meeting day and night to launch a war against Saddam Hussein, met with me to get a briefing on a code in the Bible that revealed the future.

They were under orders from the architect of the Iraq war, the Deputy Secretary of Defense, Paul Wolfowitz. But I tried to convince them that Iraq was the wrong target, that the danger remained the terrorists who attacked on 9/11, Al Qaeda.

"I don't think the real danger is Saddam Hussein, but Osama bin Laden," I told the Admirals and Generals.

"Of all the information we've found in the Bible Code one thing stands out as most useful—a clearly stated location where Bin Laden, the headquarters of Al Qaeda, and all of their most dangerous weapons might be found."

There was a stunned silence. "That would be useful," said the most senior official present, Admiral Jake Jacoby, the Director of the Defense Intelligence Agency.

It was the first time I had given American intelligence the name of the hide-out where the code stated Al Qaeda would eventually have nuclear weapons.

"There's one problem," I said as the hour-long meeting came to an end. "I can tell you where to look, but not when. I've never seen anything as clearly encoded as the name of this terrorist base, but the code does not state a year."

Professor Rips and I had not yet found "starting 2006" or the end date "2011" with "Bin Laden" and "Atomic" and "Khan".

But Admiral Jacoby, who was chairing the meeting, was unfazed.

"If you looked at Normandy one day it was just a beach," he said. "If you looked the next day it was D-Day."

It seemed like he had just given our military intelligence command its orders—target our satellites on the location the Bible Code named, and don't stop looking until you find it.

As I walked down the steps of the Pentagon I felt certain that I had accomplished my mission. I had been at the center of the inner sanctum of the invisible government. I had met with its leaders, and they had believed me.

But in a month the American military was in Iraq, and all of our intelligence resources were focused on Saddam Hussein, not Osama Bin Laden.

———

I TURNED BACK to the CIA.

In July 2006 I called the last man I had seen at the CIA, its third ranking official, Buzzy Krongard. I told him that the Israelis may have confirmed the exact place Al Qaeda already had nuclear weapons.

The Agency was in turmoil. Its longtime Director had been forced out, taking the fall for Bush over the lie the White House had told the American people—that we had to go to war in Iraq because Saddam Hussein had weapons of mass destruction.

The disgraced CIA Director had famously told the President, "It's a slam dunk."

Now a new Deputy Director, a respected veteran of the CIA was coming back, and Krongard told me he could arrange a meeting.

"But my advice is that you stick with the Israelis," he said. "From what you tell me it seems what's required is a smart, small operation. That's what the Israelis do well and we never have."

"Besides, the CIA is a mess now, and no one is going to be able to get it up and running for years."

I asked Buzzy to take a shot, make the call.

On July 26, 2006 I met with Deputy Director Stephen Kappes at CIA headquarters in Langley, Virginia.

It was his second day on the job. Kappes was legendary at the CIA, the man who had once before been in charge of the kind of covert actions you see in the movies, except of course in real life it never goes quite as well as it does in Hollywood.

But Kappes did negotiate a deal with Muammar Kaddafi, when Libya gave up its nuclear weapons program in 2003, and that revealed a world-wide nuclear black market set up by the rogue Pakistani scientist A.Q. Khan.

I had with me a 100 million to 1 code matrix that named Khan as the source of the weapon in the hands of Al Qaeda. Given that, and Israel's satellite confirmation of the dot in the desert the code named as an Al Qaeda base, I thought this meeting would be a "slam dunk."

Kappes, a grey haired ex-Marine who still had a military buzz cut, thanked me for coming to help, for being a "Good American."

But that was the high point of the meeting.

He immediately asked me a series of questions about the code, all of which I recognized as coming from random postings on the Internet. It was obvious to me that Kappes had simply Googled the Bible Code.

"If you Googled the CIA you'd find out that your Agency killed Kennedy and was behind 9/11," I said. "If you don't believe that's true, then you probably want a better source for your information about the Bible Code."

"But the code itself is irrelevant," I added. "All that matters is whether you can confirm what it states, and since it states who, what, when, and where, you can do it."

Less than 15 minutes after the meeting had started a secretary appeared and told Kappes that the White House was calling.

"I obviously have to take this call, but let me ask you a question before I leave," said Kappes.

"If the Bible is thousands of years old then how can words like 'atomic' be in it? How can there even be a Hebrew word for 'atomic'?"

I was dismayed. Kappes did not even understand the ABC's of the code.

It told the future. "Atomic" was encoded just as every detail of 9/11 had been. With all the resources of the CIA at his command Kappes had instead relied on the Internet.

"Hebrew is not just the language of the Bible," I explained. "It's also the language of a modern state that has atomic weapons and therefore, obviously, has a word for 'atomic.'"

"I have to take this call," said Kappes, "but please tell my people how 'atomic' can be in the Bible." With that, Kappes disappeared and I didn't see him again until the very end of the hour and a half meeting with his staff.

They were hopeless. I tried to explain that what was encoded in the Bible was different from the Bible itself. That it revealed modern events, that words like "atomic" appeared because nuclear terror was the danger.

I just handed them the code matrix that had in it both "New York" and "atomic." It stated the danger was in "2011."

O IN NEW YORK ☐ ATOMIC ☐ 5771 = 2011

It had no impact. None of the agents could read Hebrew, and it was obvious they still did not believe me.

"We really should be focusing on the danger," I again suggested, "because we may not have time to save New York and Washington."

"Are you telling me the code actually says 'New York' and 'Washington'?" one of the three agents asked. "How can that be in the Bible, and how could that be in Hebrew?"

"The same way we write 'Jerusalem' in English," I replied.

The three agents stared at me blankly. I realized it had never occurred to them that Jerusalem was a Hebrew name. They had been reading the Bible all their lives in English and assumed Jerusalem was an English name.

The CIA never even tried to confirm the Al Qaeda base in Yemen. I contacted Senator Edward Kennedy, and he asked the Director of National Intelligence why.

In response Kappes stated that the CIA had found no evidence to support my claim. He never mentioned that the CIA never tried to find any evidence, never looked at all.

———

"WHAT IF GOD wants to destroy the world?"

Seated across the desk from me was General James Clapper, the man in charge of all the American spy satellites that orbit the Earth. It was January 3, 2005, still the Bush years.

I was trying to make an end run on the Pentagon and CIA, both still entirely focused on Iraq. Clapper was Director of the National Geospatial Intelligence Agency. He ran our eyes in the sky that take real-time pictures of everyone and everything, everywhere, that might be a threat to the United States.

We met for two hours, and it was all business right up until the end when the General suddenly asked his surprising question.

"If we use this code to prevent our destruction," he asked, "are we interfering with God, are we thwarting His will?"

I was shocked by his Apocalyptic mind-set. I had feared that Clapper
would dismiss me as a religious doomsayer, but instead the General was the
true believer, I believed only in the code.

"I'm not religious," I told Clapper. "I don't believe in God—"

"No?!" asked the General. Now he was shocked.

"But the famous Israeli scientist who discovered the Bible Code is deeply
religious, and he believes that the code, like the Bible itself, comes from
God," I continued, reassuring Clapper.

"If you believe the Bible comes from God—"

"I do," said Clapper.

"Then I think you must believe that the code also does, because the code
is inherent in the Bible."

"Therefore," I concluded, "by using it we are not thwarting God's will, but
fulfilling it."

"It's logical," said the General.

In the Bush years everyone, everywhere in the U.S. government was religious, mainly Evangelical. The President himself was a born-again Christian. We were a theocracy, the religious right had taken over, and the word
"Bible" opened nearly every door.

But there was a downside. For example, Clapper, who would soon be promoted to Undersecretary of Defense and control 80 percent of all American
intelligence, the General who was supposed to protect us from nuclear terror, was preparing for Judgment Day.

I did not know that when our meeting began. I was in the most advanced
intelligence center in the world, and feared I would seem to its director like
a prophet of doom.

"The danger is immediate," I told the General. "We're in the End of Days
right now."

The words of Biblical prophecy were jarring to me, even as I spoke them.
Clapper, however, did not react at all.

The General never questioned that the real Armageddon might be found
using a code in the Bible that told the future. He just wanted more details.

"I read your book," said Clapper, referring to my original Bible Code book
that 10 years before had made the code and the danger known to the world.

"I hope it doesn't come true this time," he added, concerned.

I told the General our mission—to find Osama bin Laden and his nuclear weapons.

And I told him my plan—to use the 3000 year old Bible Code to target the most advanced spy technology in the world against the world's most dangerous terrorist with the world's most dangerous weapons.

I gave Clapper a code print-out. "Bin Laden" appeared with "mega-terror" and "United States."

O   MEGA-TERROR   △   BIN LADEN   □   UNITED STATES

Clapper ordered his chief satellite analyst to search for the Al Qaeda base named in the code.

Right before Thanksgiving, on November 23, 2005, Clapper and I met again. He told me his satellites had not yet confirmed the terrorist base.

I reached across the desk and handed him a new set of computer print-outs from the original text of the Bible. The danger was detailed in ancient Hebrew characters.

"'America' is encoded with 'nuclear' and 'atomic' and 'terror'," I told him. "'Suicide bomber' is encoded with all three."

I had Clapper's full attention now. "The mathematician who discovered the Bible Code calculated the odds," I told him. "It's at least 10 million to 1."

"Do you have any idea how difficult it is to re-target a spy satellite?," asked Clapper. "We have a whole world to watch."

"It names the exact place Osama bin Laden will be found," I said.

I handed the General a series of computer print-outs that gave him the name of a remote desert hide-out crossing "Bin Laden."

On one of the code tables the hidden text of the Bible said, "Army Head-quarters in X."

"I'll be sticking my neck way out," said Clapper.

I showed him another code table with a matrix that named the same place, coupled with a chilling warning: "From hide-out X terrorism will be coordinated."

It was crossed by the original words of the Bible that said, "In the End of the Days."

"I'll be going completely outside the chain of command," said Clapper.

I showed him two more code tables. The first named the same terrorist base, crossed by "Atomic" and "War." The second said "Atomic Weapon," and again named the desert hide-out.

"How will I explain this to the Pentagon?" asked Clapper.

I gave the General a new code matrix. It warned explicitly of an "atomic terror attack" on the United States. In fact, "USA" appeared twice, and the two encodings crossed each other.

ס ל ש א ל י כ ה נ ה ג ה ו ב ו ש י י ע י ב ר ר ו ד ו ה ב נ ו
ה ו ב א מ י נ א ה ט ס כ מ ה ו מ א * ו ה י ו ס ה ל ש ל ס
ח ק ל ו ש א ה ש א ה ל ע ת מ ז נ ה ו ל ו מ א י ו ה ל י
ע ת ל א ו ו ע נ ה ל א ד ד י ח ל ש ת ל א ר מ א י ו י נ
ל א ו ב ד ה כ ו מ א ל ו ת ח א ה ק ב ר י ר ב ד ת א ו ע
ס י ל ה א ב ש י ס ת ש י א ב ק ע י ו ה ד ש ש י א ד י צ
ש ע י נ ב ה ז ה ת א ו מ א י ו ו ה כ ר ב י ו ת ו ע ש ו
י מ צ ע ד א נ ב ל ו ל ו מ א י ו ה ל א ה ס י ו ב ד ה ל
ק ע י ל א * ו ה י ו מ א י ו ס ו ש ל ש ל נ מ ת כ ו מ ע
ו ב א י ב א י * ל א ב ק ע י ו מ א י ו ה ע י ל פ ל ו ר א
א ב ו ב ש י ו ו נ ת א ס ה ס י מ ל ש ה ל א ה ס י ו ש נ א
ו ו ש ד ה נ ע י נ ב ה ל א ו ו י ב א ו ו ע ב צ ל ס י ר
ת ה ל ע ד י מ ח ה נ ה ו מ א ל ו מ ת ל ד ג י ו ה ת נ מ
י מ י ת ש ל ש ס י ל ס ה ת ש ל ש ו נ ו ת פ ה ז ו מ א י
ו צ ו א ה ל כ ב ב ע ו ה ק ז ח י כ ף ס ו י ל א ו ב ש ל
ל כ א ו ב ש ל ה ל ח ת ב ו נ ד ו י ד ו י י נ ד א י ב ו
י נ ב י ת א י נ י ע ו ת ו א ו ס כ י נ י ע ה נ ה ו ד ל

○ ATOMIC TERROR ATTACK   △ UNITED STATES   ☐ UNITED STATES

"What do you want me to do?" asked Clapper.

"Prevent it," I said.

"But God might want the world to end," the General replied, again worried that he might upset a Divine plan.

Clapper paused to reflect, perhaps to seek higher guidance.

"I'll do it," he said. "We'll look, and we'll keep looking."

Clapper clearly believed that the mastermind of the Holy War against America, on the loose since September 11, 2001, might be found using an ancient code in the Bible.

He did not question that the code could help prevent a nuclear terror attack.

Once more, I left a meeting with our secret government believing the mission had been launched.

But I later discovered that no one in American intelligence, with more advanced spy satellites than the rest of the world combined, could find what the Israelis found in two weeks with just one satellite—the Al Qaeda base in Yemen.

In fact, no one in American intelligence could find what I could on Google Earth.

After the failed Christmas bombing, on December 30, 2009, I sent a letter to Clapper at the Pentagon, where he was now chief of all U.S. military intelligence. "It's more important than ever now," I told him, "because it's in Yemen"—the country where Al Qaeda had trained the bomber. Clapper never responded.

In June 2010, James Clapper, the General who did not want to interfere with God's plan to destroy the world, was promoted again, this time by President Obama.

He is now the National Intelligence Director, America's top spymaster.

At his Senate confirmation hearing July 20, 2010, Clapper was questioned sharply, following the publication of a two year *Washington Post* investigation that confirmed my own ten year experience.

"The government has built a national security and intelligence system so big, so complex and so hard to manage, no one really knows if it's fulfilling its most important purpose: keeping its citizens safe," the Post reported.

American intelligence had also become "so secretive" that no one knew what it was doing, or if it worked at all.

General Clapper, quoted in the story, said, "There's only one entity in the entire universe that has visibility—that's God."

CHAPTER   SIX

THE MOSSAD

AT A BUILDING with no name, on an unmarked road, in a place that does not officially exist, I met March 20, 2009, with the Chief of the Mossad, Israel's top secret intelligence agency.

"You never give up, do you Michael?" asked General Meir Dagan as soon as he entered the conference room.

"At least not until you do, Meir," I replied.

Dagan and I had met three times before, although he had never met with another reporter. But at our first meeting he said, "I read your book in Hebrew, and I believe this Bible Code."

I knew that Dagan was focused on Iran, on the threat that it would soon have nuclear weapons. His job was to prevent that.

"I fear that you're focused on the second nuclear attack Israel might face, rather than the first," I said. "And of course the second doesn't matter if you don't prevent the first."

"So what have I missed?" asked the Chief of the Mossad.

"A dot in the desert of Yemen already confirmed by Aman as an Al Qaeda base," I said, referring to Israeli military intelligence.

The Mossad is more like the CIA, a secret agency that does the kind of never admitted black operations we see in the movies.

"It may be the staging area for nuclear terror attacks on Israel and the United States," I continued.

"Do you know the name of this place?" asked Dagan.

I told him, and he wrote it down on a legal pad. "It's encoded as Bin Laden's headquarters," I said, "and specifically as the place where Al Qaeda may already have nuclear weapons."

"Can you show me this in the Bible Code?" asked Dagan.

I opened my laptop and began a power-point presentation Professor Rips had set up for me.

First, only "Bible Code" appeared in the matrix. Then, right next to it, "Bin Laden." Finally, right below, "Atomic."

O BIBLE CODE   △ BIN LADEN   ◇ ATOMIC

I pushed a key on the computer again and "Al-Libi" appeared, connecting "Atomic" to "Bin Laden." Al-Libi was number three in Al Qaeda, its operations chief.

ו	כ	פ	ש	ס	ד	ב	ב	ס	א	י	כ	ה	ה	ב	ז	פ	ש	ו	ש	א	ס	ד	ל	ו	פ	כ	י
ה	ב	ס	י	ב	ש	י	ס	ת	א	ו	ש	א	ﬡ	ו	א	ה	ת	א	א	מ	ט	ת	א	ל	ו
ו	כ	ש	*	ו	ה	י	י	נ	א	י	כ	ה	כ	ו	ת	ב	נ	כ	ש	י	נ	א	ו	ש	א
ו	ב	א	ה	י	ש	א	ו	ו	ב	ו	ק	י	⟨ﬁ⟩	ל	א	ו	ש	י	י	נ	⟨ﬔ⟩	ד	ו	ת	ב
ה	ש	נ	מ	ן	ב	ו	י	כ	מ	ן	ב	ד	ע	ל	ג	י	נ	ב	⟨ﬖ⟩	ה	פ	ש	מ	ל	ת
ה	ש	מ	י	נ	פ	ל	ו	ו	ב	ד	י	י	⟨ﬗ⟩	ס	ו	י	◇	נ	ב	ת	ה	פ	ש	מ	מ
ו	ש	י	י	נ	ב	ל	ת	נ	⟦ב⟧	א	י	ש	א	ו	⟨﬘⟩	י	א	ש	נ	ה	י	י	נ	פ	ל	ו
ת	א	ת	ת	ל	*	ו	ה	⟨﬙⟩	ה	ו	נ	צ	י	◇	ד	א	ת	א	ו	ו	מ	א	י	ו	ל	א
ד	א	ו	ל	א	ו	ש	י	י	נ	ב	◇	ל	ו	ו	נ	ב	ה	ל	ה	נ	ב	ו	א	ר	א	ה
ת	א	ד	ה	פ	ל	צ	ת	ל	⟨﬚⟩	⟦נ⟧	ת	א	⟨﬛﬜⟩	ת	ל	*	ו	ה	י	ב	ה	ה	ו	צ	י	י
ב	י	ט	ב	ש	י	נ	◇	מ	ד	ת	א	ל	ו	י	ה	ו	ו	י	ת	נ	ב	ל	ו	נ	י
ת	נ	מ	ן	ת	◇	ה	נ	ה	ע	ו	נ	נ	⟨ﬁ⟩	ס	י	ש	נ	ל	ל	א	ו	ש	י	י	נ
ו	ש	א	⟨יִ⟩	ט	מ	ה	ת	ל	ח	נ	⟦ל⟧	ע	ﬡ	ס	ו	נ	נ	נ	נ	י	ת	נ	ב	א	ת	ל
א	◇	ע	ו	נ	י	⟨ﬞ⟩	נ	ה	ל	ה	נ	ב	ל	⟨ײַ⟩	נ	מ	ו	ס	ה	ל	ה	נ	י	י	ה	ה
ח	נ	ה	פ	ס	ו	ל	נ	ל	א	ש	י	י	נ	ב	ל	ב	י	ה	ה	י	ה	י	ס
ו	ס	ה	ל	ה	ל	י	י	ה	ת	ו	ש	⟦א⟧ ⟨ﬠ⟩	ט	מ	ה	ה	ל	ה	נ	ל	ע	ו	ת	◇
צ	י	ו	נ	ת	⟨ﬡ⟩	ה	נ	ע	ו	ת	י	י	נ	נ	י	ת	ב	א	ה	ט	מ	ה	ל	⟨ﬢ⟩	נ	מ
ו	מ	א	ל	*	ו	ה	י	י	פ	ל	ש	ל	א	ש	י	י	נ	ב	ת	⟨ﬣ⟩	ה	ש	מ	ו
ו	ש	א	ו	ב	ד	ה	ה	ז	ס	י	ו	ב	⟦ד⟧	פ	ס	ו	י	◇	ב	ה	ט	מ	ו	כ
ב	ב	ו	ט	⟨ﬤ⟩	ו	מ	א	ל	ד	ת	ה	פ	ל	צ	ת	ו	◇	ל	*	ו	ה	י	ה	ו	צ
מ	ת	ה	פ	ש	מ	ל	ד	א	ס	י	ש	ו	ל	ה	◇	י	י	ה	ת	ס	ה	י	י	נ	ע
ת	נ	ב	ס	ת	א	ל	ו	ס	י	ש	י	ל	⟨ﬥ⟩ ⟦נ⟧	י	י	ה	ת	ס	ה	י	ב	א	ה	ט
ב	ש	י	⟦א⟧ ⟦י⟧	כ	ה	ט	⟦מ⟧	ל	א	ה	⟦ט⟧	מ	ל	ל	⟦א⟧	ו	ש	י	י	נ	ב	ל	ה	ל
ו	ל	א	ו	ש	י	י	נ	ב	ו	ק	ב	ד	י	י	נ	י	ת	נ	ב	א	ה	ט	מ	ת	ל	ח	נ

○ BIBLE CODE ⧉ BIN LADEN ○ AL-LIBI ⧗ ATOMIC

◇ IN YEMEN FOR TERRORISM, AND KHAN BUILT

The other central figure in the nuclear terror plot, the source of the weapon, was also named in the code. I hit the key again and added an extraordinary 18 letter sequence crossing "Atomic" and "Bin Laden"—"In Yemen for terrorism, and Khan built."

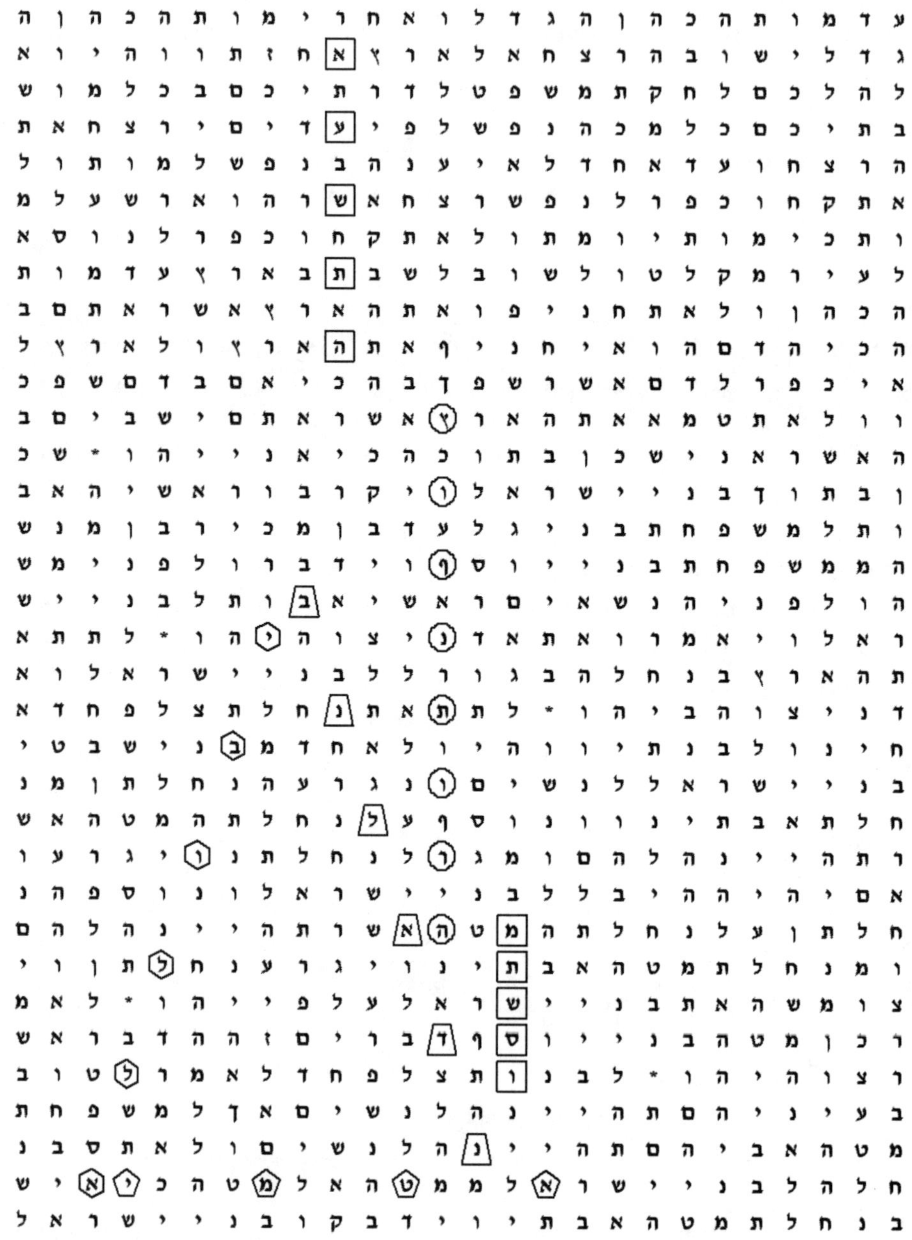

○ BIBLE CODE △ BIN LADEN ⬠ ATOMIC ⬡ AL-LIBI

□ STARTING 2006 □ 2011

A. Q. Khan, the Pakistani scientist who developed his country's nuclear weapons, and then sold the designs and the technology to build a bomb to at least three countries, Iran, Libya, and North Korea, was well known to Dagan. "It's a bad combination, Bin Laden, Al-Libi, and Khan, I think your worst nightmare," I said.

"If it's true it's not good," said Dagan. "Do you know when?"

I hit the key on my computer again, and "starting 2006" was added to the crossword puzzle on the screen. I hit the button another time and "2011" appeared.

"My guess is that nuclear weapons have been there since 2006, and that in 2011 they will attack you, if you don't attack them first," I said.

Dagan, still making notes, now very focused, asked another question, "Do you know the date?"

I pointed to the letters that appeared where "Atomic" overlapped "Mega-Terror Attack." "There are two dates, perhaps suggesting a range of time, '3 Elul' and '10 Elul,'" I said.

ל	ס	ת	י	ר	ק	ה	ו	ן	ע	נ	כ	ה	צ	ר	א	ו	ד	ר	י	ה	ת	א	ס	י	ר
ש	ס	נ	ו	ם	כ	ל	ה	נ	י	י	ה	ת	ט	ל	ק	מ	י	ר	ע	ס	י	ר	ע	ס	כ
ר	ו	ע	ה	ס	כ	ל	ו	י	ה	ו	ה	ג	ג	ש	ב	ש	פ	נ	ה	כ	מ	ח	צ	ר	ה	מ
מ	ע	ד	ע	ח	צ	ר	ה	ת	ו	מ	א	ס	ן	ס	ג	מ	ט	ל	ק	א	ל	ס	◇
ת	ת	ו	ש	א	ס	י	ר	ע	ה	ו	ט	פ	ש	מ	ל	ה	ד	ע	ה	י	נ	פ	ל	ו	ד
ה	ש	ל	ש	ת	א	ס	כ	ל	ה	נ	י	י	ה	ת	ט	ל	ק	מ	י	ר	ע	ש	ש	ו	נ

□ 3 ELUL CONFIRMATION   ◇ END 10 ELUL

△ MEGA-TERROR ATTACK   ◇ ATOMIC

In the modern calendar the Biblical month Elul usually coincides with August and September.

"And the weapons?" asked Dagan.

"That's why I'm here," I told him. "Aman has not yet seen nuclear weapons at the site, but of course that's what your enemy will keep most hidden."

"So why should I believe this?" asked the Chief of the Mossad.

"Because it's encoded against odds of 100 million to 1," I said.

"But you can forget the code, and just look at what Aman has already confirmed," I added. "Since the code is right about everything your satellite could see, I think you must assume that the code might also be right about the weapons."

"It will be difficult to confirm the weapons," said Dagan.

"It's better than the alternative," I said.

———

WHEN I FIRST stumbled across the name of the terrorist base in Yemen years earlier, I could not imagine it might be the key to winning the first battle of World War III.

In April 2002, when Israel re-invaded the West Bank, in the biggest offensive since the 1967 Six Day War, I met with the chief scientist at the Ministry of Defense in Tel Aviv, Gen. Isaac Ben-Israel.

I showed him a curious anomaly in the code. The name of a place kept appearing with every encoding of great danger, with all the likely targets of terrorist attacks.

"Where is this place?" asked Isaac.

"I don't know," I said. "There are at least two remote villages with the same name, one in Iran, the other in Yemen. Both are obviously possibilities for a terrorist base."

"You should go see General Kuperwasser," Isaac said. "He's in charge of all intelligence analysis, and will be able to find every place in the world with that name."

I met with Yossi Kuperwasser at the Kirya, the walled, tightly guarded Israeli military headquarters, in the heart of Tel Aviv.

He had already found a third place with the same name in Saudi Arabia. "All three are possibilities," said the General.

I handed him a series of code print-outs showing the suspect location with "atomic holocaust," "Jerusalem," and "Tel Aviv."

I gave Yossi another set of codes that linked the same place to "Bin Laden" and "Al Qaeda."

"We'll look at all three locations," said Kuperwasser.

But every time I checked back with him, he told me nothing had been found.

"You may be looking too early," I said. "That's the problem with the code. It's about the future."

The more closely I searched the Bible Code for the terrorist base, the more apparent it became that this place was, or would soon become the staging area for massive terrorist attacks.

It was with every danger, and it was with every target, not just in Israel, but also in the United States, most clearly with my home, New York.

Then, finally, in the summer of 2006, Rips and I found the 100 million to 1 code matrix that revealed everything. "Bin Laden," "Atomic," "Khan," and "Yemen"—all with "starting 2006."

I flew to Israel and showed it to Kuperwasser.

"Now we can look," said Yossi. "This is what you call the four W's, who, what, when, and where."

He immediately tasked Israel's satellite to search Yemen, and when he saw the photos two weeks later he asked me to come see him again.

"It's an area of terrorist activity, it's Al Qaeda, and every structure the code said would be there is there," said General Kuperwasser. "We haven't yet found nuclear weapons, but we're looking."

It was extraordinary confirmation of nearly every detail in the code. I had named a place in the middle of nowhere, a dot in the desert picked out of every place in the world, as the site where a nuclear terror attack was being planned by Al Qaeda with the help of the Kahn network.

And now Israeli intelligence had confirmed it was in fact an Al Qaeda base.

"Can you send in a ground reconnaissance team?" I asked.

"I can't authorize that," said Kuperwasser.

"Who can?" I asked.

"The Prime Minister's military advisor, General Shamni," he replied.

"Can you arrange for me to see him?" I asked.

"We're in the middle of a two-front war," said Kuperwasser.

I had arrived in Israel to find it in the middle of another war, this time with Hezbollah in Lebanon, and Hamas in Gaza, and the war was not going well.

But I pressed Yossi. "If the danger of nuclear terror is real, we're not on my schedule, and we're not on your schedule, we're on Al Qaeda's schedule," I said.

And in the middle of the Lebanon war, on August 17, 2006, I met with General Gadi Shamni, at the Prime Minister's office.

Shamni had already been briefed by Kuperwasser, so he knew that Israeli intelligence had confirmed the Al Qaeda base named by a code in the Bible. In fact, by the questions he asked I knew Shamni had read my book.

I handed the General the code table Kuperwasser had confirmed. "The famous Israeli mathematician who discovered the code said this could not appear by chance," I said.

"I'm not suggesting you take military action based on the Bible Code, but I am suggesting that given Aman's confirmation of the site as a terrorist base, you do send in a reconnaissance team to find out if there are nuclear weapons."

"We will look," Shamni said, as he stood to close the meeting. "But I will not tell you how. And any action we take will be classified."

I called Kuperwasser after the meeting. He had already heard from Shamni.

"The good news is that Gadi took it very seriously," Yossi said, "and he's already sent inquiries to all the major military and intelligence officials about the possible danger."

But Israel took no action in 2006, and there was no nuclear terror attack. Kuperwasser kept watching the Al Qaeda base in Yemen, but never found the nuclear weapons.

I was almost beginning to doubt the warning in the Bible Code myself, when Rips and I found new details. The year of danger was 2011, although the Al Qaeda plot apparently began in 2006.

The Biblical year "5771," 2011 in the modern calendar, appeared in the same who, what, when, and where code matrix that stated "starting 2006."

It was the same 6 year time span Al Qaeda took to plot, plan, rehearse, and finally execute 9/11.

- ○ BIBLE CODE   △ BIN LADEN   ⬠ ATOMIC   □ STARTING 2006
- □ YOU WILL COMPUTE THE TIME   ○ 2011
- □ ENEMIES HE KNEW, HE WILL INVADE   ⬠ TARGETS

And if there was any doubt that 2011 was intentionally encoded, that was removed by the words that overlapped the year: "You will compute the time."

Crossing the year 2011 were two possible outcomes—"enemies he knew, he will invade," and "targets."

"Targets" clearly meant the places Al Qaeda would annihilate, Israel, New York, and Washington. "Enemies he knew, he will invade" was the pre-emptive attack that could prevent it.

I flew back to Israel in March 2009 to meet with the Chief of the Mossad, General Dagan.

———

BEFORE I SAW Dagan, I met with Professor Rips.

I wanted to ask him the odds against these new details appearing in the same code matrix that had already revealed an Al Qaeda base in Yemen, the names of the terrorists, every structure at the location, and now also the years that marked the beginning and end of the plot to attack Israel and the United States.

"You can forget the code, forget the 100 million to 1 odds of who, what, when, and where being encoded," said Rips.

"Just consider the far greater, incalculable odds against it all being confirmed by satellite."

I went to Hebrew University to meet with a mathematician who had won a Nobel Prize, Robert Aumann. I showed him the same code table, and asked the same question.

"Forget the odds of the code," said Aumann. "All that matters are the odds of it being confirmed by Israeli intelligence."

"What are the odds?" I asked.

"It's incalculable," said Aumann. "Why don't we bomb the damn place?"

I explained that bombing the desert wadi and the mountains surrounding it would not destroy nuclear weapons hidden in a tunnel in one of the mountains. The only way to capture or destroy the weapons would be to send in commandos, and that could not be done until we found their exact location.

I went to see Israel's top physicist, Yakir Aharonov, who was widely expected to win a Nobel. I showed him the matrix, and again asked the odds.

"I don't know the odds of all this appearing in the code, but forget the code," said Aharonov. "Consider the odds of our satellite seeing everything the code said would be there."

"What are the odds?" I asked.

"They're incalculable," said Aharanov. "Why don't we bomb the damn place?"

I went to see the Chief of the Mossad.

"Every scientist I asked, three of the top scientists in Israel, all told me the same thing," I told General Dagan. "The odds against Israeli intelligence confirming every detail encoded in the Bible are so great they are beyond calculation. In fact, they want you to bomb the place."

"It would do no good," said Dagan.

"I know that, but don't you think it's time to send in a team of commandos?" I asked.

"It would do no good," said Dagan. "We have to know exactly where the weapons are located."

"There are two ways Israel can confirm nuclear weapons are there," I said. "Do whatever is necessary to find them, then send in commandos. Or wait until Tel Aviv and Jerusalem, along with New York and Washington, are annihilated."

"And what about the Americans?" asked Dagan.

"This is really a mission for the Mossad," I said. "You should not count on America to save Israel. I think it is far more likely Israel will save the United States."

Dagan knew it. American intelligence was in terrible shape. Nothing had changed since 9/11, except that Obama had replaced Bush, and put new people in charge of the agencies. But it would take years to repair the damage Bush had done.

"I may see the President," I told Dagan.

I gave him another code print-out. It stated "B. Obama is President."

"We found that before the first vote was cast, when Obama's election was more than improbable," I told the General.

"The President has a letter from me stating three predictions," I told Dagan.

"So the first is that he would be elected," he said. "What are the other two, may I ask?"

"The second is that his victory might cause his assassination," I said. "The third is that nuclear terror is nearly inevitable, but can be prevented."

"You don't make it easy for anyone," said Dagan. "So how does this all end, what does your code say?"

"I think that's up to us, perhaps up to you," I replied. "But I'm always the optimist, I think the good guys win."

"An optimist?" asked Dagan. "Are you a Jew?"

"It's allowed, no?" I asked in return.

"Perhaps," said Dagan. "But it's unusual."

It was a good meeting, and also unusual for the Chief of the Mossad to meet for an hour and a half with anyone.

And before I left, Dagan told me we had met despite the fact that he was not religious.

"I'll tell you a story," he said. "My father was religious, he was educated in a Yeshiva, but after the Holocaust he could not believe in God."

"I don't either, Meir," I replied. "But I do believe in the code, because it keeps coming true, and I certainly believe the Israeli satellite photographs."

"I agree with the scientists, forget the code, let's look at what has been confirmed by satellite, and find out if there are also nuclear weapons at the Al Qaeda base."

"We have our ways," said the Chief of the Mossad.

I did not ask how, but I trusted General Dagan. And I knew that President Obama might be planning a global war against Al Qaeda.

CHAPTER SEVEN

WAR OF OBAMA

"War of Obama" is encoded in the Bible with "Saving the World."

It is not what I expected, and I do not think it is what the President himself expects. Perhaps we can still avoid it.

But a major war may be the price we have to pay to save the world. It is stated over and over again in the Bible Code.

"War of Obama" is encoded with two years, "2011" and "2012." It may be right upon us.

○ WAR OF OBAMA ☐ PRESIDENT △ 5771 = 2011 ☐ 5772 = 2012 ▽ TERROR MADE CLEAR ☐ SAVING THE WORLD

"Terror made clear" appears in the same code matrix. And just below the original words of the Bible state, "Saving the World."

"It is more than 'Saving the World,'" said the Israeli scientist who discovered the code, Professor Rips. "It is 'Redeeming the World,' changing it forever, saving it permanently."

For Rips, as for every truly religious Jew, Christian, and Moslem, a war to save the world, a Final Battle between good and evil, is necessary, expected, and accepted.

For me, and I assume for Obama, it is a last resort. But a cold-eyed view of the world leads almost inevitably to the conclusion that it may be necessary.

The leading expert on nuclear terror, Graham Allison said, "We need to do today what we would not hesitate to do the day after a major city was annihilated."

If we need to fight the war, it is vital that we do it before terrorists armed with nuclear weapons wipe out Washington, or New York, or Israel, or all three, on the same day.

We will not be able to do it the day after.

"Terror made clear" must be our recognition of the danger, a pre-emptive war, not our reaction to a catastrophic loss from which the world might never recover.

I am not religious, but I believe this would be a war between good and evil, and if we lose it, the Final Battle.

———

BARACK OBAMA MAY not yet be planning to fight a global war, but the Pentagon, surely with his approval, is preparing for it.

On September 30, 2009, "the top American commander in the Middle East ordered a broad expansion of clandestine military activity to disrupt militant groups and counter threats in Iran, Saudi Arabia, Somalia, and other countries in the region," according to the *New York Times*.

The secret directive signed by General David Petraeus authorizes U.S. Special Forces to operate in both friendly and hostile nations throughout the Middle East, Central Asia, and the Horn of Africa to "pave the way for possible military strikes."

It goes far beyond the war already being fought in Afghanistan, and even the covert wars in Yemen and Pakistan.

The seven-page document specifically allows operations in Iran to prepare for war "if tensions over its nuclear ambitions escalate." The Pentagon, indeed, has "detailed war plans" in the event that President Obama authorizes a military strike.

The directive, officially called "The Joint Unconventional Warfare Task Force Execute Order," clearly lays the ground for the as yet undeclared "War of Obama" encoded in the Bible.

Its clearly stated purpose is to prepare the American military to fight Al Qaeda everywhere in the world and prevent terrorist attacks against the United States.

The war the President has not yet declared, but has obviously ordered the Pentagon to prepare for, is encoded in the Bible.

The code predicts a "Huge War," apparently the next "World War," and clearly a war on terror.

O HUGE WAR   □ IN THE END OF DAYS   △ TERRORISM   ▽ SUICIDE BOMBER

"Huge war" is encoded, with "terrorism" and "suicide bomber."

"In the End of Days" a handful of militants, even one man, can trigger the Final Battle mythologized in the Bible.

"World War" also appears with "terrorism" and "suicide bomber."

O WORLD WAR   △ SUICIDE BOMBER   ▽ TERRORISM   ☐ WAR TO THE KNIFE

World War III, as predicted in the code, will be very different from World War I and World War II. Rather than great armies colliding across the globe, it is pictured as a bitter struggle to the last man over the fate of the Earth, a "war to the knife."

And this is the war that Barack Obama may need to lead.

———

OBAMA WAS ELECTED on a promise of hope, which many took to be a promise of peace.

But the President himself always made clear that we would have to fight the terrorists who attacked us on September 11, 2001, Al Qaeda led by Osama bin Laden.

It is the real War on Terror that President Bush never fought.

"In a strange turn of history, the threat of global nuclear war has gone down, but the risk of nuclear attack has gone up," said Obama in an historic speech in Prague.

The danger is no longer the danger of the Cold War, missiles flying across the globe, wiping out everything in half an hour. Now it is religious fanatics, who want to destroy the world in the name of God, armed with weapons of mass destruction.

Al Qaeda, Obama said, is "determined to buy, build or steal" a nuclear weapon and the world is not doing what is necessary to prevent it.

"If we believe the spread of nuclear weapons is inevitable, then we are admitting to ourselves that the use of nuclear weapons is inevitable," he said.

If we fail to stop nuclear terror Obama may end his Presidency not in the White House, but in an underground bunker.

[Hebrew letter matrix grid]

○ FROM THE BUNKER   ○ B. OBAMA   ◻ MEGA-TERROR ATTACK   ◇ ATOMIC

◻ PRESIDENT SURVIVED

"B. Obama" is encoded with "from the bunker," and that is crossed by "atomic" "mega-terror attack."

"President survived" crosses "Obama," suggesting that the terrorist attack was foreseen, or even prevented by a pre-emptive attack on Al Qaeda.

But it could also mean that Washington will be annihilated, and that Obama will escape only because he is not there.

In any event, the world would change forever.

Obama and every world leader would be in underground bunkers, no matter what city was annihilated. They would have to fight an entirely new kind of World War against an invisible enemy, and do it from hiding.

O FROM RAVEN ROCK   △ OBAMA   □ THE WAR

In fact, "from Raven Rock," the name of the President's bunker, is encoded with "Obama" and "the war."

Raven Rock is more than a bomb shelter for the President. It is a vast underground Pentagon, a war room buried deep in a granite mountain six miles from the President's retreat in Camp David.

It was created at the height of the Cold War, so the surviving United States government could fight a nuclear war if attacked.

No year is clearly encoded with that Apocalyptic image, but the "Huge War," the "World War," the "War of Obama" all seem to be predicted before the end of the President's first term in 2012.

———

AFTER 9/11 EVERYONE believed what the Bible Code had predicted many years before, that nuclear terror was the greatest threat we faced. But no one did anything to prevent it.

Even after Israeli intelligence told the White House it had confirmed the exact location where Al Qaeda might already have nuclear weapons, the U.S. government still ignored it.

But the code suggests that President Obama will heed the warning on time. "Pre-emptive attack" appears with "atomic threat" and "President" "Obama."

O PRE-EMPTIVE ATTACK   □ ATOMIC THREAT   ◇ 5770 / 2010   △ OBAMA   □ PRESIDENT

There is also a year, 2010. In the ancient Biblical calendar it is "5770." In Hebrew, the same letters that spell the year, ask a question—"Will you save?"

There seems to be only one scenario that begins and ends well.

Pre-emptive attacks in Pakistan and Yemen, the first to seize the 100 nuclear weapons Pakistan has mounted on missiles, the second to capture the weapons Pakistan already gave Al Qaeda.

Obama may be planning the first right now.

"The U.S. military is reviewing options for a unilateral strike in Pakistan in the event that a successful attack on American soil is traced to the country's tribal areas," the *Washington Post* reported in late May 2010.

It was the failed Times Square attack by a Pakistani who confessed he was trained by the Taliban in the lawless tribal areas that triggered the threat of American military action.

"Obama said during his campaign for the Presidency that he would be willing to order strikes in Pakistan, and Secretary of State Hillary Clinton said in a television interview after the Times Square attempt that 'if, Heaven forbid, an attack like this that we can trace back to Pakistan were to be successful, there would be very severe consequences,'" the Post reported.

"Obama dispatched his National Security Advisor, James Jones, and CIA Director, Leon Panetta, to Islamabad this month [May 2010] to deliver a similar message to Pakistani officials."

The warning in the Bible Code is of a far greater threat from Pakistan.

O THE PAKISTANI   △ ATOMIC   ▽ TERRORIST   ◇ OBAMA   □ KHAN   □ CREATOR

"The Pakistani" "atomic" "terrorist" is encoded with "Obama."

It is an explicit statement of the ultimate terrorist attack, perhaps this time a nuclear bomb in Times Square.

And that suggests the plan to strike Pakistan only after a successful terrorist attack could be a catastrophic mistake.

There is no need to wait for proof that Pakistan's nuclear weapons are a danger to America. It has been known for years that the scientist who created the weapons, A.Q. Kahn, also sold bomb factories to Iran, Libya and North Korea, and that two scientists in his nuclear black market network met with Bin Laden right before 9/11.

Indeed, in the same matrix that warns of a "Pakistani atomic terrorist," "Khan" is also encoded with "creator."

The weapons he created are now controlled by ISI, Pakistani intelligence, which itself created Al Qaeda. In effect, Pakistan's 100 nuclear warheads are already in the hands of militants. But the immediate danger remains Al Qaeda in Yemen.

If the United States and Israel can use the Bible Code to find nuclear weapons Al Qaeda already has before they are used, a 30 man commando team can win the first battle of World War III.

An eleventh-hour victory over the ultimate terror attack is predicted in the code, at the Al Qaeda base in Yemen already confirmed by Israel.

○ IN 5770 / 2010 THEY DISCOVERED   ◻ MEGA-TERROR ATTACK   ◇ ATOMIC   ◇ YEMEN

○ USING THIS HOUR TO SUCCEED   ◻ SEIZING THE MOMENT

"Atomic" "mega-terror attack" crossed by "Yemen" appears with "in 5770 (2010) they discovered." It strongly suggests that by "seizing the moment" in 2010 we can prevent it.

The United States is already waging a covert war in Yemen but it is aimed at stopping local Al Qaeda groups, not a nuclear terror attack from Bin Laden and Khan.

But "atomic" "weapon captured" is encoded with "prevented 2010."

O WEAPON CAPTURED   △ ATOMIC   □ IN BATTLE   ◇ 5770 /2010 PREVENTED

And again it is clear that military force will be necessary—"in battle" is encoded with the surprise attack on the Al Qaeda base in Yemen.

We can win the first battle against nuclear terror, if we act pre-emptively.

Instead of a "World War," a "Huge War," the "War of Obama", a team of commandos can destroy or capture nuclear weapons in Yemen, at the dot in the desert first named by the code, then photographed by an Israeli satellite.

And that dramatic last-minute victory over Bin Laden can awaken the whole world to the global danger.

HALF OF ALL the nuclear weapons and enriched uranium in the world are now vulnerable to terrorists.

A pre-emptive attack that saves us from an immediate atomic threat would not end the danger of nuclear terror.

Winning the first battle of World War III might only allow us to fight the rest of the war, and keep terrorists from ever getting nuclear weapons again.

"Atomic" crosses "weapons secured." "In the world" appears in the same matrix.

O WEAPONS SECURED   △ ATOMIC   □ IN BATTLE   □ IN THE WORLD

But the code suggests we may not be able to lock down all the world's nuclear weapons without a fight. "In battle" again appears, crossing "atomic" "weapons secured."

We cannot kill every terrorist in the world. We cannot even find them. But we know what countries possess nuclear weapons, and we can secure all of them.

"All that the United States and its allies have to do to prevent nuclear terrorism, is to prevent terrorists from acquiring nuclear weapons," says Graham Allison, the top expert.

"Enforcement should start with political isolation and economic sanctions," he said, "but also include the readiness to use covert and overt military force if necessary."

"Confiscation of weapons" is encoded with "atomic," and "law of the world."

○ CONFISCATION OF WEAPONS   △ ATOMIC   ☐ LAW OF THE WORLD FOR GENERATIONS

But this new world order, according to the code, will likely require military action.

No one believes that Iran, North Korea, or Pakistan, will voluntarily give up their nuclear arsenals. Pakistan created a nuclear black market, North Korea is still selling nuclear designs, and Iran is the world's leading sponsor of terrorism.

"We must now move to a war on nuclear terrorism," says Allison, a former Assistant Secretary of Defense who is now a Harvard professor. He is an academic, not a warrior.

But he is a realist who understands human civilization will not survive unless we are ready to secure nuclear weapons where we can, and remove them by force where we can't.

"Nuclear" also appears with "Obama" and "to confiscate" crosses the President's name. "For the world" is encoded in the same matrix, and in Hebrew also means "forever."

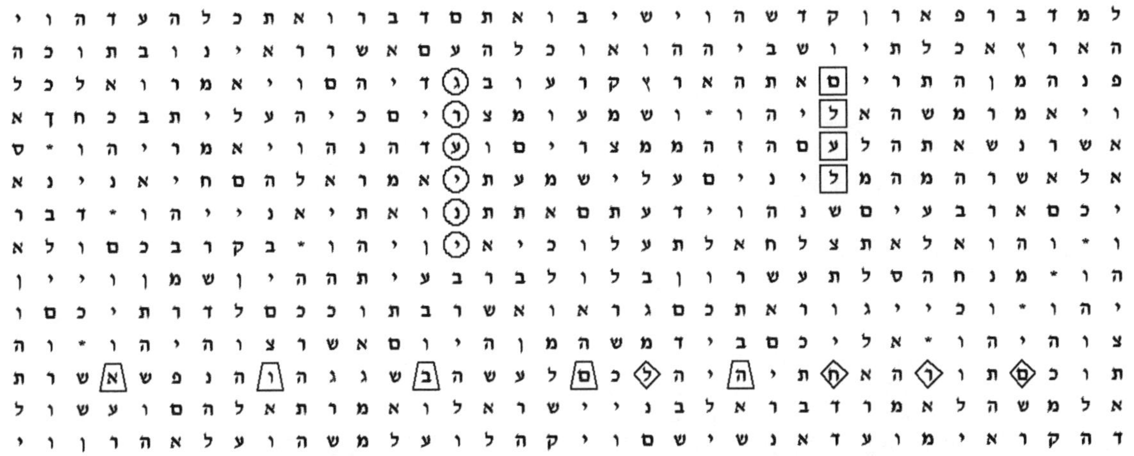

ל מ ד ב ר פ א ר ו ק ד ש ה ו י ש י ב ו א ת ה ס ת ד ב ר ו א ת כ ל ה ע ד ה ד ה ו י
ה א ר ו צ א כ ל ת י ו ש ב י י ה ה י א ו כ ל ה ע ס א ש ר י נ ו ב ת ו כ ה
פ ג ה מ ו ן ה ה ת ת א ה ת ת א ר ק ר ע י ו ב �ג ד י ה ה ס ו י ר מ א נ ל א כ ל פ
ו י א מ ו מ ש ה ת א ש ל א ה ו י א
א ש ו ר ש נ ת ה ה ל ע
א ל ש ר ה ת ה מ מ ה ל
ה ו ש א ש פ נ ה ה נ ג ג ש ה ה ש ע ל ד

○ NUCLEAR   ◇ TO CONFISCATE   △ OBAMA   □ FOR WORLD / FOREVER

The United States must lead, but cannot by itself win the global war. America and Russia have 90% of all nuclear weapons, but must join with China to create a new world order.

None of the three, especially Russia, have even entirely secured their own nuclear stockpiles.

But the greatest threat comes from the least powerful countries with nuclear capability.

And it only takes the amount of plutonium that can fit into a Coca Cola can to make a weapon that can destroy an entire city.

"On the current course, nuclear terror is inevitable," says Allison. "No one who has studied the facts doubts that another catastrophic terror attack is coming."

"If we are to avoid the impending disaster, and the consequent cascade of nuclear weapons exploding in our cities, the United States will have to engage the major countries in a global campaign to prevent nuclear terrorism now."

"By doing so, they can preserve all nations from the nightmare of a world in which nuclear terrorists destroy civilization as we know it."

"Atomic threat" is encoded in the Bible. "Very great blow" appears in the same place, but instead of a terrorist attack, it is an attack on terrorists "from Obama."

O   ATOMIC THREAT   □   VERY GREAT BLOW   △   FROM OBAMA

In fact, the Bible Code states that "Obama" from a "bunker" might have to lead "all his people to war."

"Time for battle" is encoded with "Obama" in the same matrix.

We will not escape the "atomic threat" without a fight. But we can prevent it, if we act in time.

O   BUNKER   □   ALL HIS PEOPLE TO WAR   △   OBAMA   ▽   TIME FOR BATTLE

The battle will be necessary. But it can lead to peace.

There are two ways to write "Mega-Terror" in Hebrew, they appear together only once in the Bible, and "Atomic" is encoded in the same place.

ת	נ	ו	ד	א	מ	ד	א	מ	ב	ד	ך	ת	א	י	ה	ו	פ	ה	ו	ך	י	ת	ה	נ	ס	י	ו	ג	נ	ו	מ	ה	ב	א	י
ו	א	צ	ה	ס	ע	ה	א	ב	ו	ת	ב	ל	ה	ו	ה	נ	ה	ו	ס	ו	ל	ש	ו	ו	מ	א	י	ו	ו	ל	ס	ו	ל	ש
י	מ	ל	ה	ב	ו	ס	ו	י	ל	א	ה	ע	ו	פ	ו	ב	ד	י	י	ה	ע	ו	פ	⬡ס ⬡ו ⬡פ ⬡ש	ת	א	ה	נ	י	ע	י	ס
א	י	ת	ה	ל	ש	ו	ה	ק	ז	ת	ד	י	ב	א	ל	ו	ד	ל	ה	ל	ס	י	ו	צ	מ	ך	ל	מ	ס	נ	א	נ	ת
ש	א	א	ו	ה	ס	ה	ל	א	ו	מ	א	י	ו	ה	ש	מ	ל	ו	ד	י	ג	י	ו	ה	ד	ע	ה	י	א X י ש נ	ל	כ
א	ת	א	ש	ל	ס	י	ד	ב	ל	ס	י	ה	ב	ל	ה	י	ה	ו	ו	י	ד	צ	י	נ	ש	ל	ע	ה	ו	ש	ע	ת	ו	י	ת
ע	ו	ד	י	ת	א	ך	מ	ט	ו	*	ו	ה	י	י	נ	פ	ל	ו	ב	י	ו	ק	ה	ו	ו	נ ⬡ב ⬡ו ⬡ק ⬡ז ⬡ע ⬡ס	א	ו
י	ב	ז	ה	ו	ב	ע	ג	י	ו	ש	א	ש	ו	ה	י	ל	ו	ו	ב	ו	ע	ה	ד	ע	א	מ	ט	⬡ו	ס	י	מ	ב	צ	ח
ס	כ	ה	ת	א	ו	ה	כ	ה	ו	ל	ב	ש	ח	ו	ו	ה	ד	ש	ש	י	ד	ק	י	ל	ב	י	ה	⬡ד	ה	א	ס	א	ו	ס
א	ס	א	י	כ	ך	ל	א	א	ל	י	ו	י	ל	א	ו	מ	א	י	ו	ל	א	ו	ש	י	ל	ע	ב	ו	⬡ט	ו	ז	ד	*	ו	ה
ב	ו	מ	א	י	ו	י	ה	י	י	ה	ה	ה	ת	ו	א	ו	י	ת	ג	ו	ה	ה	כ	ת	א	ס	ו	ג	⬡ה	ה	ע	י	כ	י	נ
מ	י	⬡א	ל	ו	ל	⬡א ⬡ב ⬡נ	מ	⬡ו	ל	ק	⬡א	ל	ס	⬡ו	ו	⬡ע	ה	ס	כ	ל	⬡ו	י	ה	ו	ה	⬡נ ⬡ג	ש	ב	ש	⬡פ	נ	ה
ש	א	ו	ו	צ	ו	א	ל	כ	ל	ו	ס	י	ו	צ	מ	ד	ל	מ	ה	ע	ו	פ	ל	ס	ו	י	⬡צ ⬡ט	ד	ו	נ	ה	ב	ה	ש
י	ו	ה	ז	ה	ס	ו	ק	מ	ה	ל	א	נ	ו	נ	א	ב	י	ו	ס	י	ה	פ	מ	ב	ו	ת	ו	ת	א	ב	ו	ל	ד	א

○ MEGA-TERROR ◻ MEGA-TERROR ATTACK ◇ ATOMIC ☐ PRESIDENT

▽ FROM A FIERCE BATTLE ○ PEACE

Oddly, "peace" also appears in the matrix.

It is, however, a peace that according to the code will come only "from a fierce battle" waged by the "President."

Losing the first battle of World War III, would almost certainly mean losing the entire war. We might never recover from the nightmare of nuclear terror.

The crucial question is whether we fight the battle before the nightmare — or wake up to the real Armageddon.

CHAPTER EIGHT

SAVING THE WORLD

TRUMPETS SOUNDED AS Barack Obama walked down the long aisle of the soaring ceremonial hall in Oslo, Norway, to receive the Nobel Peace Prize on December 10, 2009.

The Nobel chairman invoked the story of Martin Luther King Jr., winner of the same prize in 1964, as he turned to the President saying, "Doctor King's dream has come true."

And then Obama shocked everyone by not being King, by not preaching non-violence, but by telling the world it had to embrace the concept of a "just war."

"We must begin by acknowledging the hard truth," said the President. "We will not eradicate violent conflict in our lifetimes. There will be times when nations will find the use of force not only necessary but morally justified."

There was stunned silence in the grand hall.

"The world may no longer shudder at the prospect of war between two nuclear superpowers," Obama said, "but nuclear proliferation may increase the risk of catastrophe. Terrorism has long been a tactic but modern technology allows a few small men with outsize rage to murder innocents on a horrific scale."

This was not the speech that anyone expected. Instead of repeating his call for a "world without nuclear weapons," he spoke of the danger of a world in which even random lunatics could get nuclear weapons.

"I face the world as it is," said the President. "Make no mistake, evil does exist in the world."

A new kind of warrior had just accepted the Nobel Peace Prize. And it was all encoded in the Bible 3000 years ago.

ט ו א ת א ב י ו נ ו ה י ו ס ו ה א ח ד א י נ נ י י נ ו ו י א מ ר
א ו ב נ א ל א ב י ו ל א מ ר ו א ת ש נ ב י ו ת מ י ת נ א ס
י י ו ו י ו ר י י ו ו נ נ ב ח ל ה ל ה (כ) ש ב נ ו א כ ל ו י ה י כ י ב
ח נ ו נ ה י ה ל א ד נ י י ל ע (נ) ד י ו מ א נ ו ד ג ס ע ת ה
ע ל י י ו ו י ק ר א ה ו צ י א (ה) כ ל א י ש מ ע ל י ו ל א ע
ה י ו ס י י ב א ו א ר ו צ כ נ ע (ו) ל א ע י ק ב א י ה ס ו י ו
ע ק פ ב כ ל ס נ פ ש ש ב ע ה ל כ ל (ה) ו פ ש ה ב א ה ל י ע ק ב מ
ף ה ה נ ו מ צ א ב א ר צ מ צ ר י ו (ס) ו נ א ר צ ו נ ע י ו ב ש ב ר
ת א פ ר י ו ס י ו ל ג ד ל י ע ק (נ) ו י א מ ר ה נ ה ב נ ד י י ו נ
י ו ק ר א י ע ק ב ל א ב נ י ו י (ו) י א ו מ ר ה ה ת א ס פ ו ו נ א ג
ו ת א נ צ ח נ ק י ו א נ ר ב ק פ ה (א) ש ת ו ו ש מ ה ק ב ק ב ה ת י א
ש נ ו ס י ו א ר נ א י ו ס פ ל א [פ] ר י ו ס ב נ י י ו ש ל ש י ו ג ס
ב נ ג ר מ א נ נ מ ו ה ב נ ח מ [ר] ו ב נ פ ת ו ט ס ב ה ה נ א ת
ר ה נ ס ו ה ר י י א ר נ ה ה י ה [ס] נ ה ע ב נ ר א ש ו ה י ה ס נ ה
ת י א ש ר ו א ע ש ו ה ק ב ר ו נ [ו] א ח ר י כ נ ו י ש ל ש א ת נ כ
ס ב י ד ד נ מ ר י ה נ ו * א ל מ ש ה ב ל כ ת ד ל ש ו ב
ק כ ס ל ל ב נ כ ר ה ת מ ל ש ו נ [מ\נ\ל\ש] ל ש ו ג ס ח מ ל ג ס ה י ו ס
מ ו נ י ה א ד ר ו י י ו צ ח ו ר ו ש א ו ל ב נ ה כ נ ו ע נ
א נ ס פ ר ע ה ל כ ח מ כ ו ס ו ל כ ש פ י ס ו י ע ש ו נ ג ס

O OBAMA NOBEL   **☐** HIS PRIZE   **△** PEACE

The code matrix was perfect. "Obama Nobel" appeared with "his prize" and "peace."

It had been foreseen thousands of years before, although the *New York Times* reported that it "stunned people from Norway to the White House."

And "Obama Nobel" with "peace" was repeated in a second code.

There its larger meaning was also stated, "In order to prolong your days on Earth."

○ OBAMA NOBEL   ◇ PEACE   □ IN ORDER TO PROLONG YOUR DAYS ON EARTH

Outside the hall in Oslo as the President received the prize a crowd chanted and held up a yellow banner reading, "Obama you won it, now earn it."

What neither the crowd inside the hall nor outside understood is what the President did, and tried to tell them—in the real world there are times that the only way to achieve peace is through war.

———

FOR ALMOST 15 years I have been trying to warn world leaders that the ancient prophecy of an Apocalypse was about to come true, that the real Armageddon is encoded in the Bible.

Now, finally, a world leader has appeared who might actually be able to perform a near miracle—and prevent it.

○ SAVING THE WORLD   △ OBAMA WILL MAKE REAL   ◇ WITH A CODE

◇ 5770 = 2010 = WILL YOU SAVE?

"Saving the World" is encoded in the Bible. "Obama" and "with a code" appear in the same place, with the year 2010.

In Hebrew the same letters that spell the year, also spell a question—"Will you save?"

Seen at first as an almost Messianic figure, Obama always tried to make it clear he does not walk on water.

But he is President at a defining moment in world history, that may determine if we survive.

Can President Obama defeat a hidden enemy more dangerous than Hitler, in just two years?

The far greater probability stated in the code is that the danger will last through 2011 and 2012, to the end of Obama's first term. But it need not end in a global cataclysm.

"To save the world" and "life on Earth" appears with "war" and "2011."

○ TO SAVE THE WORLD　　□ LIFE ON EARTH　　△ WAR　　◇ 5771 = 2011

The code clearly says Obama can prevent Armageddon.

"He will save the world" is encoded with "Obama" and "President" exactly where "powerful" "atomic" "weapon" also appears, with a year, 2012.

It is not stated as a question, but encoded as the answer.

צ א צ י ל כ ה ה ל ע מ ו ה נ ש ס י ר ש ע ן ב מ ת מ ש ר פ ס מ ב
נ ב ו ו נ ח י ו כ ש מ ל ב י ב ס ו ו ה ת ר ש י ס ה ו ו י י ל כ
ק פ ו ו א ב צ ו ר ו צ ה ד פ ן ב ל א י ל מ ג ה ש נ מ י נ ב ל
ת ו ה כ ת א ו מ ש ו ד פ פ ת ו י י נ ב ת א ו ן ר ה א ת א ו ל
פ ש מ ל ב א ת י ב א י ש נ ו ס י ת א מ ו ס י פ ל א ש ש ה ל
ו ה ו ו ה נ ח מ ה ע ס נ ו י י י נ ב ו ו ר ה א א ב ו ס י ש ד ק ה
ה ת ח פ ש מ ת ב ע ת א ז ד ע ו מ ל ה א ב ה ד ב ע ד ב ע ל א
ש ל ש ס ת ח פ ש מ ל ס ה י ד ק פ ו י ה י ו ד ע י מ ל ה א ה
מ ו ו ר כ ז ת ח נ מ א ו ה ת א נ ק ת ח נ מ י כ ה נ ב ל ו י ל
ס י ב נ ע ת ר ש מ ל כ ו ה ת נ ש י א ל ו כ ש צ מ ח ו ו י י צ מ
ל א י ו ה י נ ב ד י י ו ר ז נ ת ר ו ת ל ע ה ש ש ע י נ כ ר ד י
מ ה א מ ו ס י ש ל ש ת ח א ף ס כ ת ר ע ק ו נ ב ר ק ת א ב ר ק
ש ב ה ל ו ל ב ת ל ס ל ס י א ל מ ס ה י נ ש ו ד ק ה ל ק ש ב ל ק
כ ד ח א ל י א ו ק ב ן ב ד ת א ו פ ת ו ט ק ה א צ מ ב ה ה ז ה ר
ד י ו ס י ב ו כ ה י נ ש ו י ב מ מ ת ד ע ה ו ר א ל ע ר ש א ת ר
ו ל א ר ש י י י ב ס ה ה ל ו ש ע ו כ ס י ו ל ל ה ש מ מ א י ו ה
ו ג ס כ ת א ו י ג י י כ ו א ו ה ה ש י א ה א ש צ ו א נ ט ח ו ד
ל א י ו נ פ ל ו ו ר כ ז ל ס כ ל י י ה י ס כ י מ ל ש י ח ב ז ל
מ א י ה ח נ ב ר ד י י נ מ ד י א נ ש מ ו ס ו י י ו ד י ב י א ו
ס ה ת ל כ א ו ו ש ב ס כ כ ל * י ה י י נ ת נ י ס י ר צמ ב ו ו נ ב ל ב
א ת י ש כ ה ה ש א ה ת ו ד א ל ע ה ש מ ב ו ה ר א ו ס י ר מ ר
א ג ד ה ט מ ל י ס פ ו ו ב י נ ב ח י י ל ת פ נ ה ט מ ל ל א כ
ל פ נ ה ו מ ק נ ע י י נ ב ס י ל י פ ו נ ה ת א ו ו נ צא ר ו ס ש ו ת
ח ל ד ג כ ה ה ז ה ס ע ה ה ו ו י ע ל א ו נ ח ל ס ס ו י ע ב ר ל ע ו ס י

○ HE WILL SAVE THE WORLD △ OBAMA □ PRESIDENT ◇ WEAPON

□ POWERFUL □ ATOMIC ◇ 5772 = 2012

The Bible Code echoes what Obama stated in Oslo, but on a scale so great it is only captured by the words of Biblical prophecy.

Seizing nuclear weapons Al Qaeda may already have, stopping terrorists from ever getting nuclear weapons again, will require military action, perhaps the ultimate war for survival.

"Saving the World" appears with "in the End of Days," crossed by "terrorism."

O SAVING THE WORLD   □ IN THE END OF DAYS   △ TERRORISM

□ WAR   □ WAR

Again, echoing Obama, the awful necessity is "war."

So, it is not a promise of Divine Salvation, it is not a promise of an easy peace, but a statement that we, here on Earth, can save ourselves.

Perhaps with the help of the Bible Code.

"I HAVE ONLY one reason to believe the world will survive," said the scientist who discovered the Bible Code, Eliyahu Rips.

"God's promise, the Creator's promise after the Flood never to destroy the world again."

He was quoting Genesis, God's promise to Noah:

"I will make My covenant with you, and all life will never be cut short by the waters of a Flood. There will never again be a Flood to destroy the Earth."

"I have placed my rainbow in the clouds, and it will be a sign of the covenant between Me and the Earth."

It was March 2009. I was in Israel to see the Chief of the Mossad, but first met with Professor Rips at his home in Jerusalem. For me the subject was nuclear terror, but for Rips, as always, it was God.

I asked Rips if he believed God's promise not to destroy the world was also a promise not to let us destroy the world.

Rips told me he had never considered the question before. "It is an interesting nuance," he said. "Does the promise of the Creator also include preventing mankind from destroying itself?"

I had no faith at all in God's covenant, or the rainbow, but I did have faith in mankind.

"I believe that mankind will decide its own fate," I said. "I do not think it will be easy, and I do not think our victory will come without a price, but I do think we will survive."

Our entire discussion was at once in a religious context, about the "End of Days," and at the same time the real world danger of Armageddon, nuclear terror.

I mentioned a theory that all intelligent species everywhere in the universe would self-destruct. It was first stated by the astronomer Carl Sagan, the first prominent scientist to suggest that intelligent life existed beyond our planet—a theory now accepted by almost all scientists.

Sagan said it was inevitable that at some point all intelligent life forms would create the means to destroy themselves, as we have, and then would eventually do so.

I believed, from the Bible Code and world events, that we were right now in that deciding moment of human history. So do most experts on nuclear terror. So does President Obama.

I wished I had Rips' faith in a God who would save his creation.

"Everything in the world happens with a kind of supernatural supervision," said Rips. "It is intentionally hidden, behind the scenes, so we just don't know."

I asked him about free will, quoting an ancient commentary on the Bible, the Talmud: "Everything is foreseen, but freedom of action is granted."

For almost 2000 years great sages have debated the apparent paradox, always in religious terms—how can there be human free will if God knows what will happen in advance.

The Bible Code makes that question real for the modern world, even for those like me, who are entirely secular. How can the future be known, yet changed?

"Free will of course exists," said Rips, "but it is just one of the players on the field."

Since it was the only player I could deal with, I kept trying to use the Bible Code to persuade world leaders that we right now faced the greatest danger the world has ever faced, but we could change our future.

I looked for "Changing the Future" in the code. It appeared just once—in a place that amazed me.

O CHANGING THE FUTURE   △ IN 5770 = 2010   O SAVING

□ AS A SIGN OF THE COVENANT BETWEEN ME AND YOU, THE RAINBOW

Right above "Changing the Future" were the very words of Genesis that Rips had quoted to me a year earlier:

"And God said, 'This is the sign that I am providing for the covenant between Me and you, and every living creature. I have placed My rainbow in the clouds, and it shall be a sign of the covenant between Me and the Earth.'"

The covenant, the rainbow—I was shocked. Suddenly all my skepticism was challenged.

I was already writing the end of this book, had stated my disbelief in God's promise, when I searched the Bible Code for "Changing the Future."

Suddenly, displayed on my computer screen, was the answer.

"Changing the Future," our way to save ourselves, was clearly intentionally linked to God's promise not to destroy the world.

Was Rips right? Did it all come back to God?

I felt almost as if He was watching over my shoulder as I wrote, saw my lack of faith in Him and the rainbow, and through the code was responding to my skepticism.

I told Rips that anytime it seemed like the code was speaking to me, that God was speaking to me, it made me uncomfortable.

"You are not the first person for whom this is uncomfortable," said Rips. "Adam was also very uncomfortable with it."

I never actually believed that God or the code was in contact with me personally. But often it felt that way—as if I was on-line with the Encoder.

I asked Rips if he ever felt like it was a dialogue taking place in real time.

"Always," he said. "Even though you are asking the questions 'now,' and the Bible was encoded in the distant 'past,' from the point of view of the Encoder, it is all happening at once—including the 'future' He is revealing through the code."

It was not only Rips, a religious man who believes in an eternal God, who can imagine that time is simultaneous. It is also what Einstein said:

"The distinction between past, present and future is only an illusion, however persistent."

For me, however, there was a clear difference between yesterday, today, and tomorrow. And whatever higher reality might exist, in our world time was running out, fast.

The code was clearly intended for this moment. "Changing the Future," encoded in the Bible just once, crossed this year, 2010.

It could not be by chance. Our moment to save our world, to change our future, was now.

———

IN FACT, "SAVING" was encoded parallel to "changing the future."

I asked Rips if he thought the change would come from us, or from God. "It is not clear if man will do it with God enabling it, or it will be done entirely by God," he said.

The very existence of the Bible Code suggested a partnership. Obviously, the code did not come from one of us.

Rips was certain it came from God, because the Bible itself came from God. All I could be sure of was that it came from another intelligence, I hoped one trying to help us survive.

Certainly we needed to change our future.

I looked for another way of stating the same thing—"He will change the future." Remarkably, it appeared with "In the End of Days" and "Peace."

O HE WILL CHANGE THE FUTURE ☐ IN THE END OF DAYS Δ PEACE

The code clearly stated at least the possibility of a peaceful future, instead of an Apocalypse. The End need not be the end.

The original Hebrew could in fact be read two ways—"In the End of Days," the end of the world, or "in the Latter Days," our own era, this moment in time, the future foreseen 3000 years ago.

"He will change the future." It predicted a good outcome in a time of great danger.

But who was "He"? Was it God? Or was it man?

If it was not a partnership between man and God, it was at least a partnership between us and the Bible Code.

So I kept trying to tell world leaders what the code revealed.

An accident had put me in a very odd position. I was telling the people who ran the world the future, they often believed me, but did not know how to change it, what to do.

Every time I meet with a President, a Prime Minister, the head of an intelligence agency, there were always two questions.

"If it's predicted what can I do?" they asked me.

I'm always expecting disbelief and instead hearing resignation. I always tell them it's a warning, not a prediction, that what we do, what they do, can change the future.

But there is always a second question. The people who run the world turn to me and ask, "What should I do?"

That's the question that scares me. It's like I'm in the cockpit with the pilot at 30,000 feet and he suddenly asks me, "Do you know how to fly this thing?"

I'm just a reporter. And the code only reveals information, not solutions.

The code did not come with an instruction book. Or, if it did, we have not yet found it. I had no magic powers, no Messianic illusions. I had been a reporter since I was twenty and still saw myself as a reporter, just one who had stopped telling what had happened yesterday, and was now instead telling what would happen tomorrow.

I could not change the future by myself.

Still, what had been hidden in the Bible for 3000 years, now revealed by computer, was the key to our survival.

IN THE BIBLE Code, both the code itself and President Obama are foretold as the two keys to winning the real battle between good and evil in the End of Days.

"Obama" appears again with "he will save the world," but the same matrix also states "code he will see."

O HE WILL SAVE THE WORLD △ OBAMA ▽ CODE HE WILL SEE ☐ PRESIDENT ☐ 5770 / 2010

Will the President, with the code, save the world?

"The world will be saved," predicts the Bible Code, but only by a "very great blow" "from Obama"—the exact words encoded with "atomic threat."

O THE WORLD WILL BE SAVED ☐ VERY GREAT BLOW △ FROM OBAMA ☐ 5770 / 2010

Even with the help of the code, President Obama may have no choice except the one he invoked when he won the Nobel Peace Prize, a "just war."

The "War of Obama" that the Pentagon has been planning since September 2009, is no longer just a plan.

U.S. Special Forces already have boots on the ground in 75 countries, according to a June 2010 *Washington Post* report.

"Plans exist for pre-emptive or retaliatory strikes in numerous places around the world," the Post stated.

The White House has openly stated that America will not wait for a terrorist attack, but will "take the fight to Al Qaeda."

"World Peace" is also encoded in the Bible. It is crossed by "in order to prolong your days on Earth." "He will save" appears in the same place.

There is hope.

O WORLD PEACE   □ IN ORDER TO PROLONG YOUR DAYS ON EARTH

◻ ALL HIS PEOPLE TO WAR   O PRESIDENT   □ HE WILL FIGHT   □ HE WILL SAVE

But in the same matrix again the harsh reality that we may have to fight for "World Peace" is very clear.

"All his people to war" is also encoded, and "President" "will fight" appears just above.

Obama himself has stated that the next few years will determine the fate of the world.

The threat is not only nuclear terror, it is all the dangers we now face. The President remains in danger of assassination, and it is Obama's destiny to prevent nuclear terror. If we lose even one major city, there will be no economy.

It is one world. Everything is intertwined. But there remains one overriding danger.

We will either prevent nuclear terror, stop religious zealots from destroying the world in the name of God, save our great cities, or human civilization will not survive.

No one leader, not the code itself, will save us. It will be the whole world acting as one.

And the clock is ticking down fast toward Armageddon.

CODA

CODA

I THOUGHT I could do it without magic. But now it seemed to be perhaps the only solution, short of war.

I was focused on warning President Obama of a nuclear terror attack threatened by Bin Laden, what the leader of Al Qaeda himself called "an American Hiroshima."

But as much as I tried to escape what always seemed to me too fantastic to be true, the Bible Code kept drawing me back to a "Code Key," the magical object necessary to unlock the code completely, see our entire future clearly.

The code states again and again that it is buried in a peninsula that juts out into the Dead Sea from Jordan, named "Lisan."

I've walked the ground, a totally barren moonscape that shines white in the desert sun. It is a place that seems straight out of mythology, the lowest land on all the planet, the navel of the Earth, that ancients said connected us to the supernatural.

For 12 years I had been trying to launch an archeological expedition to dig up the Code Key, but in the Middle East even archeology is made impossible by the politics of religion.

So I had put it aside. In any event, my search for the key had seemed irrelevant in the face of nuclear terror.

But the Bible Code would not let go. It repeatedly took me back to the key, until I realized it might be the only solution.

"This is the solution" appears just twice in the original words of the Bible.

The words are spoken by the best known fortune-teller in the Old Testament, Joseph.

Sold into slavery by his jealous brothers, Joseph rose to become the virtual ruler of Egypt by telling the Pharaoh the future.

But his words—"this is the solution"—also appear in the Bible Code with "Atomic Terror Attack," and again with "Bin Laden."

And crossing "this is the solution" each time it appears is the name of the barren peninsula at the Dead Sea, "Lisan."

○ ATOMIC TERROR ATTACK　　□ THIS IS THE SOLUTION　　△ LISAN

"Atomic Terror Attack" is encoded only once in the Bible, and "this is the solution," and "Lisan" cross it.

"Bin Laden" is also encoded with "this is the solution" and "Lisan."

The danger we face today—an "Atomic Terror Attack" by "Bin Laden"—appears with both "this is the solution" and "Lisan" in a 3000 year old text.

בש ר ו א ב ל א ו ד ח י ו כ ל י י ו ו מ ק י י י י ו ר ע נ ג ל א ם ה ה ר ב
ו ד ל ו ח ק ד י נ פ ל ה ק ב ה ר ה נ ה ב ו ט ו א ע ו ד י י ל א ר ב ד
י ח א ל ש י א ו ע ב ש י י ו ר ק (ב) ב ו מ י כ ש י ו ו ת ש י י ו ל כ
פ ל ע ו ב א ה ת א ו ב י ש ה ו (ו) א צ ה ת א ו ק ש ה ו ר א ב ה י פ
ה כ ס א י ד מ ע ע ו ה ל ס י * (ל) א ו נ ת נ א ל ו ס י נ מ ת ו ש ע
י ל א ו מ א י י י נ ת כ ו ב ס (א) י כ ד ח ל ש א נ ל ר מ א י י ו ה ח
ב ל א ו ש י נ כ ש ב י ה י י ו ר (ו) ע ל ד ג מ ל ה א ל ה מ ה ל ה נ א ט
ו ה ו י י כ י ו א ל ס א א י ה ד (ו) ב ת נ ת כ ה א נ י ו ה ו נ א צ מ
י ת ש ל ש ס י ל ס ה ת ש ⟦ל⟧⟦ש⟧⟦ו⟧⟦נ⟧⟦ו⟧⟦ה⟧⟦פ⟧⟦ה⟧⟦ז⟧ י מ א י י ו ף ס ו י י ו ע
ד ו נ ח ב י י י ו ס א ה ס ת א ו ס כ י ח א ת א ח ק י י ד ח א ס כ
פ י ו ס ש ו נ ד י ע א ו ה ו ף ס ו י י ה ת י ב י י ח א ו ה ד ו ה י

O BIN LADEN   ☐ THIS IS THE SOLUTION   △ LISAN

That could not happen by chance.

———

MY QUEST FOR the key that would unlock the code completely had started in Professor Rips' small cramped study at his home in Jerusalem.

He said that the Bible Code was like a giant jigsaw puzzle, and we had only a handful of the pieces.

"Do you think we will ever be able to see the code whole?" I asked.

"If we ever get the key," said Rips.

Every code has a key. It's how a military or spy agency sends a secret message that can only be read by its intended recipient.

But what was the key to the Bible Code?

Rips believed the code came from God. I didn't know what to believe, but clearly it did not come from one of us.

One night I opened my laptop and searched for "Code Key" in the Bible. What appeared was more than a surprise.

"Obelisks." It was not what I had expected to find crossing "Code Key." I had imagined a mathematical formula, or a set of instructions, not a physical object, much less Obelisks.

ו ז ו נ ח ת א ד ל ת ו ר ה ת ו ו ת ש א ת א ן י ק ע ז י

ו ת ב ת א ו ף ל ד י ת א ו ש ז ל פ פ ת א ו ו ז ח ת א ו ד

ק מ ב ה ב צ מ ב ק ע י ב צ י ו ו ת א ו ב ד ו ש א ס ו ק

ת ב א ס ש ו י מ ש ס ה ב א ו ק י ו ס י ר ע נ ה ת א ד ו

ו י ב ו ל ד ג מ ו י ב ת ו י ח ה י פ י ו פ ל ו נ ח י ו

ת ת נ ו ו י ע ר כ ו ו ב ר ק ת צ ח ר ו ו י ח ת נ ל ח ת

ל ע ה ח ב ז מ ד ו ס י ל א ד פ ש י ו פ ה ס ד ל כ ת א ו

ז ה ת י ה ו ר פ כ י ל ה ק ה ס ע ל כ ל ע ו ס י נ ה כ ה

ש מ ח ו ס י פ ל א ת ע ב ש ס ה י ד ק פ ה ל ע מ ו ש ד ח

ש ב ס ע ה ל כ ל י כ ס כ ו ת ב ר ג ה ו ג ל ו ל א ר ש י

O CODE KEY   ☐ OBELISKS

I had seen Obelisks, tall stone pillars that came to a pyramid shaped point. There were some 100 feet tall, 4000 years old, that still stood in Egypt, engraved with hieroglyphics telling the deeds of ancient Pharaohs.

But what did they have to do with the Bible Code?

There was no doubt the encoding was intentional. "Obelisks" appeared with "Code Key" twice, both times actually crossing it. Rips told me the odds against that were a million to one.

"No other pair has had such high statistics in the history of code research," he said. "Two direct hits could not happen by chance. That is mathematically certain."

But the code stated a lot more. These Obelisks were not merely stone pillars, but in some way oracles. They told the future.

Both times "Obelisks" cross "Code Key" the original words of the Bible state a phrase, "Mouth of the Obelisks." And there was another phrase, even more mysterious, "Lord of the Code."

Lord of the Code. Was that God? Or was that some intelligence beyond my imagination, but less than the Creator.

It could be a Biblical way of saying "Master of the Code," in other words, the unknown "Encoder."

O CODE KEY   △ MOUTH OF THE OBELISKS   ▽ LORD OF THE CODE

Perhaps on a barren peninsula at the Dead Sea was buried the physical proof of the Bible Code, but far more than that.

The object might also reveal the source of the code, who it came from. But it would be even more than that.

It would be the first physical evidence we've ever had that we're not alone.

The cosmic potential of this archeological adventure was irresistible.

Still, it was hard for me to believe that ancient Obelisks were the key to the code, much less the key to our survival, the way to stop the real Armageddon, nuclear terror.

In any event, only a call from the White House to the King of Jordan was likely to end 12 years of futile efforts to dig up the "Code Key," the "Obelisks" in Lisan.

So I searched the code for "Obama Obelisk," and found something more than remarkable.

"OBAMA TO COORDINATE Obelisk with you" appeared as a single uninterrupted code matrix.

```
ם  י  מ  ש  ה  ף  ו  ו  ע  ל  כ  ל  כ  ת  א  ו  ה  ד  ש  ה  ת  י  ח  ל  כ  ה  מ  ד  א  ה  ן  מ
י  מ  ט  ע  מ  א  נ  ח  ק  י  ד  ד  ב  ע (ל) ע  מ  ו  ב  ע  ת  א  נ  ל  א  ז  י  נ  י
ד  ש  ל  א  ו  ד  מ  א  י  ח  א  נ  ב  ל (ה) ו  נ  ב  מ  ה  ש  א  ס  ש  מ  ד  ל  ח  ק
ס  י  ז  ע  י  ד  ג  ח  ל  ש  א  י  כ  נ (א) ו  מ  א  י  ו  י  ל  א  א  ו  ב  ת  י  כ
ו  ס  י  ו  פ  א  ש  א  ו  ל  ע  ו  נ  י (מ) י  ד  י  י  י  ב  א  ת  י  ש  י  י  כ  ף
י  מ  י  ת  ש  ל  ש  ס  י  ו  צ  מ  ץ  ו (א) ל  כ  ב  ה  ל  פ  א  ד  ש  ח  י  ה  י  ו
ת  ט  ו  נ  ל  ב  ו  ל  ע  ה  נ  ע  ת  א  ל (ו) ת  ע  ו  ל  ס  י  ב  ו  י  ו  ת  א  ה  י
ה  ל  א  ו  ק  ב  ב  ת  י  ל  ע  ו │ר│ק│ב│ל│ו│ו│כ│נ│ ה  י  ה  ו  ת  ו  ב  ש  ו
כ  ד  כ  ו  ע  ב  ו  א  צ  ה  נ  מ  ס  י (מ) ת │ל│ י  א  *  ו  ה  י  ל  ו  מ  ש  א  ת
ב  ט  ס  ב  כ  י  ה  ב  כ  ש  מ  ב  ע  ג  ו (ה) ל │כ│ ו  א  מ  ט  י  ו  י  ל  ע  ב  ש  ת
ה  ד  ש  ה  ת  י  ח  ת  א  ס  כ  ב  י  ת (ח) ל │ש│ה  ו  ס  כ  י  ת  א  ט  ח  נ  כ  ע  ב
א  ו  ב  ו  ק  ה  ז  ה  ש  מ  ח  ה  נ  ו  ש (י) נ │ב│ ס  י  ש  ב  כ  ה  ש  מ  ה  ס  י  ד
ו  ק  י  ו  ש  א  ו  ש  ב  ל  כ  ל  ס  ם  ח (נ) ו  ט  פ  ל  כ  ה  י  ה  י  ד  ל  ל  א  ו
ש  ה  ס  ו  י (ב) ו  ס  ה  ה (ו) כ  ס  ו (ה) ה  נ  ח (נ) מ  ו  ד  י  מ  ת  ה  ה  נ  ל  ע  ת
ם  כ  ל  י  נ  ת  ה  נ  ו  ש  א  ס  כ  י  ו (ע) ב  ו  ב  ש  י  ס  כ  ל  ב  ד  ה  נ  ק  מ
ו  ד  ל  ו  ת  נ  ו  ו  ו  פ  א  נ  ו  ו  ח (מ) *  ו  ה  י  ב  ו  ש  י  נ  ע  מ  ל  ס  ו
ל  ש  מ  ל  כ  ב  ו  ו  ד  י  מ  ס  א  ב  ה (ס) ו  ב  ב  ה  ת  א  ד  ת  א  *  ו  ה  י  ו  צ
```

○ OBAMA TO COORDINATE OBELISK WITH YOU

△ CERTAIN TO VISIT / EXAMINE   □ WITH INTELLIGENCE

⬠ INTELLIGENCE AGENCY

Would Barack Obama really join my search for the Obelisks?

Rips calculated the odds. They were 40 million to 1 that the 16 letter sequence would be encoded by chance.

Neither Obama nor I existed when the Bible was written. And yet the code named him, and seemed to be answering my questions in real time. It was at once beyond belief, and mathematically beyond chance.

Obama himself had to see this extraordinary matrix.

And on the very code table that a year in advance stated his election, "B. Obama is President," everything about my stalled archeological adventure also appeared.

"My code" "on key" and "obelisk" all were encoded with the prediction that "Obama" would be "President."

O B. OBAMA IS PRESIDENT △ OBAMA ☐ PRESIDENT ⬡ MY CODE ▽ ON KEY

O OBELISK

It was as if the prediction was not only foretold in the code found by computer, but already foreseen, even destined in the Code Key engraved on the ancient Obelisk.

And "Obama" appeared again with the "Obelisks" in a code that suggested the key would explain his improbable victory, perhaps even foretell his re-election.

"Obama" is encoded with a matrix that in Hebrew has two very different, yet entirely clear meanings: "Election explained," and "on Obelisks explained," crossed by "President" twice.

O   ELECTION EXPLAINED / ON OBELISKS EXPLAINED   △ OBAMA

☐ PRESIDENT PRESIDENT   ▽ CODE   ☐ MY CODE   ☐ ANCIENT

"My code" and "ancient" appear in the same place, and so does the promised explanation—"he threaded a needle, he slipped through a narrow opening."

It was perfect. Obama had indeed slipped through an opening that barely existed.

On stone pillars thousands of years old, buried in the peninsula at the Dead Sea, a modern triumph as miraculous as any story in mythology may be perfectly stated.

A black man became President of the United States in perhaps the only moment in America it could have happened, in the aftermath of the collapse of the Bush Presidency, in an election that was determined by the collapse of the economy in its final weeks.

And now I needed Obama to fulfill the promise of the code, to help me find the key to the code.

It could be the ultimate intelligence tool, an object that would reveal our entire future—in time to change it.

———

WITHOUT A MIRACLE we might not survive.

The "key," the "obelisks," appeared again with "mega-terror."

O MEGA-TERROR   □ LISAN, TONGUE OF SEA   △ ANCIENT KEY / MAP OF SENSOR

▽ MAZRA   □ OBELISKS

So did the exact location, the peninsula in Jordan, "Lisan," and the exact spot on the peninsula, a tiny village, "Mazra." In ancient times it was a port at a small inlet of the Dead Sea and that too was encoded, "Lisan, tongue of sea."

Crossing the precise location, on the matrix with "mega-terror," appeared the words "ancient key," and the same letters in Hebrew also spelled "map of sensor."

In the 3000 year old code was a treasure map, and instructions on how to use it.

The enemy, "Al Qaeda," was also encoded in the Bible in a matrix that again suggested the obelisk would help defeat it.

"From obelisk he blocked" appears with both "Al Qaeda" and the danger, "terrorism."

O AL QAEDA   ⌂ FROM OBELISK HE BLOCKED   ☐ TERRORISM

The "battle" to eliminate the immediate "atomic threat" from Al Qaeda was stated as a "prophecy on the Obelisk."

Again it was not merely a prediction encoded in the Bible, but on its key, on an Obelisk so ancient that no record existed of it, except in the code.

O ATOMIC THREAT BATTLE   △ PROPHECY ON OBELISK

Finally, the ultimate answer to the global threat, "atomic" "weapons secured" also appeared with the same words that were originally found with "Code Key"—"Mouth of the Obelisk" and "Lord of the Code."

It was all far beyond chance, far beyond easy imagination, but mathematically certain.

With "Atomic Threat," with "Mega-Terror," with "Al Qaeda," and with the answer to all three also appeared a detailed statement of my archeological adventure.

O WEAPONS SECURED   △ ATOMIC   □ IN BATTLE   □ IN THE WORLD
O MOUTH OF THE OBELISKS   O LORD OF THE CODE

Perhaps it really was, as the fortune-teller Joseph said, "the solution."

"SAVING THE WORLD" appeared with the Code Key, the object from beyond our world that would allow us to see our world as if through the eyes of God.

O SAVING THE WORLD   △ KEY   ▽ TABLET MAZRA   □ LISAN   □ I WILL SAVE   △ KEY

"Key" was encoded twice with "Saving the World" on a matrix that once again stated the exact location.

A promise, "I will save", appeared with "Lisan," the name of the peninsula in Jordan, and again the precise place, "Mazra."

"Saving the World" was encoded again with "key."

As stated here, Professor Rips told me, it was not merely saving the world but redeeming it, saving it permanently.

And in the same matrix the Code Key is stated as the very source of our salvation—"You saw from Key."

And here, too, was the ultimate statement of the battle that might be necessary, "War of God."

O SAVING THE WORLD   △ YOU SAW FROM KEY   □ WAR OF GOD

War of God. I could not believe in the very concept. But everything about the Bible Code, everything about the Code Key, defied everything I could believe about the world.

And yet there is no question the code is real. In fact, I had no doubt that its key was buried exactly where the code states, and that we could use it to help save our world.

I had hoped that the Code Key would lead us all to a peaceful solution. Instead, it seemed to state there would be no peace without war.

The key might still be "the solution," but to stopping nuclear terror, to winning the first battle of World War III.

In the real world, inhabited by both Barack Obama and Osama bin Laden, survival might require more than magic.

As Winston Churchill famously said on the eve of World War II, it might require, "Blood, sweat, and tears."

Can Obama be Churchill? Can he be Roosevelt?

This whole book, which begins with a letter to Obama, is an open letter to the President.

He may need the code, even the key, to save the world.

NOTES

CHAPTER NOTES

PROFESSOR RIPS USED the standard Hebrew language text of the Bible, known as the *Textus Receptus*, in his Bible Code computer program, the basis for the code research cited in this book.

The software I used was developed by Rips and his computer programmer Dr. Alex Rotenberg.

All Torahs—the first five books of the Bible in Hebrew -- that now exist are the same letter for letter, and cannot be used if even one letter is wrong.

The best-known edition of that text, *The Jerusalem Bible* (Koren Publishing Co., 1992), contains the most widely accepted English translation of the Old Testament, and is the primary source of quotes from the original text in this book.

I have also consulted and sometimes used a translation some scholars prefer by Rabbi Aryeh Kaplan, *The Living Torah* (Maznaim, 1981).

Quotes from the New Testament are primarily from the King James Version, although I have also consulted a modern translation known as the New International Version.

The statements by Rips quoted throughout this book come from a series of conversations I had with him over the course of seven years, primarily at his home in Jerusalem and in his office at Hebrew University, and in hundreds of telephone interviews.

Many of the events described in the book were witnessed by me. Accounts of other events are based on interviews with persons directly involved, or were confirmed by published news reports.

The events encoded in the Bible use the same Hebrew that appears in the plain text of the Bible, or the same Hebrew used by Israelis today.

The names of people and places are taken from standard reference sources like the *Hebrew Encyclopedia*. The Hebrew spellings for more current events are those used by Israeli newspapers, mainly *Ha'aretz*.

The translations of all encodings have been confirmed by the authoritative R. Alcalay Hebrew-English dictionary (Massada, 1990) and the standard unabridged Hebrew dictionary, A. Even-Shoshan (Kiryat Sefer, 1985).

The years encoded in the Bible are from the ancient Hebrew calendar, which starts in Biblical times, 3760 years earlier than the modern calendar. The current year, 2010, is roughly equivalent to the Hebrew year 5770. But Biblical years begin in September or October, according to the lunar calendar, and end in September or October of the following year.

All of the Bible Code matrixes displayed in this book have been proven to be encoded beyond mathematical chance. The statistics are calculated automatically by the Rips-Rotenberg computer program. The computer scores the matches between words using two tests — how closely they appear together, and whether the skips that spell out the search words are the shortest in the Bible.

The odds of all the most important codes, all that are stated to appear at odds beyond 10,000 to 1, were calculated by Professor Rips, using more advanced software.

All of the odds stated tell how unlikely it is that the words, names, places, dates, would appear together by chance in the Bible. The code does not tell us how likely it is that the predictions will come true.

But there does appear to be a clear connection between the odds of the event being encoded, and the event happening. As I've told world leaders, it would be foolish to ignore warnings of great dangers that appear in the Bible far beyond chance. They too often come true.

Each code word determines how the computer presents the text of the Bible, what crossword puzzle is formed. The original order of the letters is never changed.

For example, "B. Obama is President" appears only once in the Bible with a skip of 1404. So the computer divided the entire original Bible—the whole strand of 304,805 letters—into 217 rows of 1404 letters. The Bible Code print-out (p. 4) shows only the center of that code table.

If "B. Obama is President" was spelled with a skip of 100, then the rows would be 100 letters long. If the skip was 1000, then the rows would be 1000 letters long. And, in any event, the rows are stacked one on top of another, never changing the original order of the letters in the Bible.

Three thousand years ago the Bible was encoded so that the prediction "B. Obama is President" would appear once, exactly where "Obama" and "President" appear again, with the month he was elected.

The opening quote from Albert Einstein was stated by him shortly after World War II, in May 1947, and was published in *The New Quotable Einstein* (Princeton University Press, 2005, p. 173). I first saw it in an exhibition of his original handwritten Theory of Relativity on display at the Israel Museum, in Jerusalem.

The quote from The Talmud, an ancient commentary on the Bible, on the co-existence of free will and foreknowledge is attributed to Rabbi Akiva (*Mishna Avot* 3:15).

For almost 2000 years sages have debated the apparent paradox—how can there be human free will if God knows everything in advance? The Bible Code poses the same question, even for the secular. The answer appears to be what science states—that there are only probabilities, that there isn't just one future, but many possible futures. We determine the outcome.

CHAPTER ONE: OBAMA

THE MAY 28, 2008 letter I sent Barack Obama through Oprah Winfrey was confirmed sent by Oprah's personal assistant, Libby Moore, June 5, and confirmed received by Obama's best friend and closest advisor, Valerie Jarrett, in a telephone conversation with me a few days later.

I sent it to Oprah with a cover note predicting Obama would be President, but warning of a possible assassination attempt. My letter to Oprah stated,

"I think I can only help Senator Obama if I reach him directly—I can't, but you can."

I never fully believed the Bible Code's prediction of Obama's election, found before the first primary, which I discussed with Professor Rips in December 2007, until CNN declared him the winner the evening of Election Day, November 4, 2008.

When I watched Obama claim victory, just before midnight, in a speech to 100,000 people in a park on the waterfront in Chicago, I had the sense that he could barely believe it. I saw Oprah in the crowd, crying.

The quotes of his speech were transcribed as he spoke, and confirmed by the report in *The New York Times*.

The *Times* was also my primary source for reports on the Presidential race, although I also routinely checked *The Washington Post*.

I first heard about the Bible Code by chance in June 1992, after meeting with Gen. Uri Saguy, who was then Chief of Israeli Military Intelligence.

I first met with Dr. Rips at his home in Jerusalem in late June 1992. The Gulf War encoding he showed me that night was originally found by his colleague Doron Witztum. Rips confirmed that Witztum told him the date of the first Scud missile attack on Israel, and that Rips himself saw it encoded in the Bible, three weeks before the Gulf War started.

Chaim Guri met with me at his home in Jerusalem September 1, 1994. He called Rabin's office that night, and the next morning the Prime Minister's driver picked up my letter warning of the encoded assassination, and delivered it to Rabin. The letter was dated September 1, 1994.

Rabin was murdered at a peace rally in Tel Aviv on the evening of November 4, 1995. Yigal Amir, a 26-year-old Orthodox Jew, fired three shots, hitting Rabin twice in the back. The code predicted the murder a year in advance, and stated the Biblical year Rabin was killed. It also named his assassin in nearly every encoding, but we could not see it until we knew the name.

The events of September 11, 2001 were witnessed by me, and the details were confirmed by news reports in *The New York Times*, *Time* and *Newsweek*. I did not see any immediate television coverage, because all the broadcasts I received came from the World Trade Towers.

Dr. Rips sent me by e-mail the same Bible Code table I found minutes after the towers fell, but the telephone lines were blocked, and it did not reach me until the next day. What was most striking to him, as a mathematician, was that the three words anyone would automatically look for, "Twin" and "Towers" and "airplane" were encoded together in the same place against odds of 10 million to 1. In Israel, the World Trade Center is known as the "Twin Towers," also the name in *The New York Times* headline.

Rips' original experiment was published in *Statistical Science* in August 1994 (Vol.9, no.3), pp.429-438, "Equidistant Letter Sequences in the Book of Genesis," Doron Witztum, Eliyahu Rips and Yoav Rosenberg. It reported that the names of 32 rabbis who lived after Biblical times matched the dates of their birth and death in the Bible Code against odds of 4 in a million. In a series of later experiments the actual odds were found to be 1 in 10 million.

John Podesta, Chief of Staff at the White House told me that President Clinton had my book with him at Camp David, when he met there in July 2000 with Yasir Arafat and Ehud Barak. I met with Podesta in the White House October 16, 2000.

My letter to President Bush was dated August 3, 2001, and I called the White House September 10, 2001. I was told that his Chief of Staff Andrew Card and his National Security Advisor Condolleeza Rice both received it.

Sir Isaac Newton's search for a code in the Bible was described in an essay "Newton, the Man" by the famous economist John Maynard Keynes (*Essays and Sketches in Biography*, Meridian Books, 1956). Richard S. Westfall, in *The Life of Isaac Newton* (Cambridge University Press, 1993, p.125), also quoted Newton's notebooks, and stated that the physicist "believed that the essence of the Bible was the prophecy of human history."

In Rips' statement that Newton could not find the code because it was "sealed until the time of the End," he is quoting from the Book of Daniel 12:4.

The legendary original form of the Bible dictated to Moses by God—"contiguous, without break of words"—was stated by the 13th century sage Nachmanides in his *Commentary on the Torah* (Shilo, 1971, Charles Chavel, ed., Vol. I, p.14). The continuity of the Bible is also expressed in its traditional form as a scroll, one continuous parchment that is unrolled.

The U.S. National Security Agency codebreaker Harold Gans told me the results of his independent experiment in two telephone interviews, January 1993 and December 1996.

Gans stated the odds of also finding the names of the cities encoded with the names of the rabbis were 1 in 200,000.

When I first found the prediction that Obama would be President in December 2007, before the first primary in Iowa, I called Rips at his home in Jerusalem, and he, like I, immediately saw that "he was assassinated" appeared in the same place. In fact, the danger was intertwined with nearly every prediction of Obama's victory.

The first prominent public report that top people in the Obama campaign feared assassination appeared in *The New York Times* February 25, 2008.

Barbara Walters asked the President-Elect about it in an interview just before Thanksgiving 2008, and CNN openly stated the danger in its coverage of Inauguration Day, January 20, 2009.

Obama's Inaugural address was transcribed as I watched it and confirmed by *The New York Times*.

I first spoke to Valerie Jarrett by telephone March 12, 2008 and sent her a letter for Senator Obama March 14, which she sent to the Secret Service.

I sent a new letter to Obama May 28 by fax to Oprah Winfrey who contacted Jarrett and I spoke again to Jarrett on June 10. The next day Jarrett sent me an email "re: Senator Obama / Secret Service," stating, "I did contact the head of Barack's detail immediately after we spoke."

On June 18 I sent her a memo "Preventing Obama Assassination" and followed it with another August 14, that both stated details, a profile of the potential assassin, and how he might attempt a murder, the latter stressing that Obama might be in danger when he accepted the Democratic nomination at an open football stadium in Denver, August 28.

Right before Jarrett left for the Democratic Convention, August 22, I sent her a new email, "I'm trying to help the Secret Service save Senator Obama's life. However busy you are preparing for the Convention, please don't leave out the most important step, doing everything you can to make sure the Senator survives." That same day I got a call from Secret Service headquarters in Washington confirming that my memos had been received from Jarrett.

I finally spoke to Richard K. Elias, the Assistant Director for Intelligence at the Secret Service September 18, 2008. He had clearly read my memos, he noted each key detail, and although he refused to meet he did assure me that everyone at Secret Service headquarters, and everyone protecting Obama in the field had the information I sent through Jarrett.

When I stated that "the Secret Service has never prevented an assassination," Elias did not dispute it but simply said "we're way better now" than the last time a President was shot, Ronald Reagan in 1981. Elias did not mention that the Secret Service still uses a 1980's mainframe computer, as reported on *ABC News* February 26, 2010.

Reagan was not saved as many think by the Secret Service. He was actually pushed into the line of fire by the agents protecting him. It did not become known for years but the chief of Reagan's surgical team said he almost died on the operating table.

In the same September 18, 2008 conversation Elias agreed that Obama would be in greater danger the closer he got to the White House and would remain in danger as President.

In fact, assassination threats against Obama spiked after he was elected, before his Inauguration, and in the early months of his Presidency, according to *The New York Times*, December 6, 2009.

The Secret Service reported that threats to kill Obama after he became President jumped 400 percent, *In the President's Secret Service*, Ronald Kessler (Random House, 2009, p. 282). Also see "The Guns of August," Frank Rich, *New York Times*, August 23, 2009, for a report of even more open threats that began with the rise of the Tea Party.

CHAPTER TWO: NUCLEAR TERROR

THE BIBLE CODE states that Al Qaeda already has nuclear weapons, and names the exact place, which I revealed to American and Israeli intelligence but obviously will not reveal in this book because that would help the terrorists rather than the officials trying to prevent the attacks.

Every top government expert, including President Obama, states that Al Qaeda is seeking nuclear weapons. Rolf Mowatt-Larsson, a 23 year CIA veteran who led its task force on Al Qaeda and WMD issued a report January 25, 2010 stating Bin Laden continues his pursuit of nuclear weapons. FBI Director Robert Mueller stated the same in congressional testimony March 17, 2010.

Obama's 47 nation nuclear security summit took place in Washington April 12-13, 2010, where the President restated that Al Qaeda was seeking a nuclear weapon "and if they ever succeed, they would surely use it," according to *The New York Times*.

The *Times* report also quoted White House Counter-Terrorism Advisor, John Brennan, about Bin Laden's meeting with Pakistani nuclear scientists.

I first contacted Brennan by fax at his White House office December 30, 2009 right after the failed Christmas bombing by a Nigerian trained by Al Qaeda in Yemen.

My fax to Brennan stated, "I have information that may be urgent for the White House to have about Al Qaeda in Yemen, already confirmed in large part by Israeli intelligence, but not known to American intelligence."

I followed with a phone call to Brennan at home January 3, 2010 and as he asked arranged a call from General Yossi Kuperwasser, who confirmed the exact location I stated as an Al Qaeda base by satellite when he was Israel's chief intelligence analyst. Kuperwasser called Brennan's White House office January 6, 2010. Brennan sent a CIA official from the American Embassy in Israel to see Kuperwasser a week later but never contacted him again.

On March 5 I faxed Brennan stating, "I just spoke to General Kuperwasser, who told me he has satellite photographs of the site in Yemen that may be our best lead to nuclear weapons Al Qaeda already has."

Brennan never requested the satellite photographs from Israel, he never contacted Kuperwasser, and he never replied to me, nor did he answer the two questions I asked him in my March 5, 2010 fax: "(1) Is U.S. intelligence following up on Israel's lead?; (2) Will you request the satellite photographs that prove the information I provided Israel is entirely accurate?"

Rips and I found the "Bible Code," "Bin Laden," "Atomic," "Khan," "Yemen" matrix at his home in Jerusalem, and Rips calculated the odds against it all appearing in a few verses of the Bible as at least 100 million to 1. He said it was mathematically impossible to be encoded together by chance.

The description of the impact of a possible nuclear terror attack on Washington is based on several expert reports, including *Nuclear Terrorism*, Graham Allison (Henry Holt, 2005), *The Fate of the Earth*, Jonathan Schell (Knopf, 1982), and a series of reports from the Belfer Center at Harvard's Kennedy School of Government, and the Nuclear Threat Initiative directed by the former Chairman of the Senate Armed Services Committee Sam Nunn.

The quoted statement of a 9/11 Commission panel that a nuclear terror attack is likely "by the end of 2013" was published in an authorized edition of the report, *World at Risk* (Vintage Books, December 2008, p. xv).

The official name of the expert panel is the Commission on the Prevention of Weapons of Mass Destruction, and the report was officially sent to President Bush and Congress December 2, 2008, with a cover letter stating "the sobering reality is that the risks are growing faster than our defenses, our margin of safety is shrinking, not growing."

My letters to President Bush warning of the same danger stated in the code were dated August 3, 2001, more than a month before 9/11, and October 1, 2001.

Allison's statement that Al Qaeda spent 6 years planning the 9/11 attacks, and would likely take at least as much time to plan a nuclear terror attack is quoted from his book *Nuclear Terrorism*, p. 216.

The Bible Code stated the danger of nuclear terror long before 9/11. I told Israeli Prime Minister Shimon Peres when we met on January 26, 1996 at his office in Jerusalem. He had never recognized the danger before, but just days later on January 30 made a speech in Jerusalem stating that the greatest danger facing the world was that nuclear weapons would "fall into the hands of irresponsible countries, and be carried on the shoulders of fanatics." It was reported in the *Jerusalem Post* January 31.

My first Bible Code book, published in 1997, stated exactly what President Obama said at his nuclear summit in April 2010, that "instead of a nuclear war between superpowers the world may now face a new threat—terrorists armed with nuclear weapons." *The Bible Code*, (Simon & Schuster, 1997, p. 127).

After September 11, 2001 everyone recognized the danger. The first *9/11 Commission Report* stated, "The greatest danger of another catastrophic attack in the United States will materialize if the world's most dangerous terrorists acquire the world's most dangerous weapons." (Authorized Edition W.W Norton, p. 380).

I warned President Clinton of the danger in a letter dated July 5, 2000 and his Chief of Staff Podesta confirmed July 17 that he gave my letter and a copy of my book "directly to the President at Camp David." As stated earlier I warned President Bush in two letters August 3, 2001 and October 1, 2001.

Thomas Kean, Chairman of the 9/11 Commission was quoted stating, "We have no greater fear than a terrorist who is inside the United States with a nuclear weapon," in a *New York Times* report November 15, 2005.

The same *Times* story quoted the full Commission in its final statement saying, "We believe that the terrorists will strike again."

My letter to former President Clinton dated October 21, 2005 stated, "We need to do today what we would do on the day after an entire city is wiped out." It was given him through his former Chief of Staff Podesta, who tried with me to convince Clinton to get himself appointed special envoy to deal with world leaders to prevent nuclear terror by President Bush. Clinton agreed in principle, then said no without stating a reason, and instead earned $7.5 million in speaking fees in 2005.

Obama's speech in Prague stating, "The spread of nuclear weapons or theft of nuclear material could lead to the extermination of any city on the planet," was reported in *The New York Times* on April 5, 2009.

Years before a senior CIA official told me on background, "If Al Qaeda doesn't already have nuclear weapons they're incompetent."

A former White House official told me that the leading expert on nuclear terror, Allison, had told him almost exactly what Rips said to me, "It may take the destruction of a whole city to wake up the world."

Allison's statement, which has become Obama's policy, "All the United States and its allies have to do to prevent nuclear terrorism is to prevent terrorists from acquiring a weapon," is stated in his book *Nuclear Terrorism* (p. 15).

Former Senator Nunn, director of the Nuclear Threat Initiative stated that Russia and the United States have most of their nuclear missiles pointed at each other on five minute hair-trigger alert in a documentary *Nuclear Tipping Point*. Both his organization and Allison's Belfer Center at Harvard have estimated there are 25,000 nuclear weapons in the world, and that Russia and the United States have 90 percent of them.

Bin Laden's plan for "an American Hiroshima" was stated in the *9/11 Commission Report*, p. 380. The same report stated Al Qaeda had tried to acquire nuclear weapons for at least 10 years.

The sealed letter I gave my lawyer Michael Kennedy that stated two predictions, a global economic collapse, and nuclear terror, was dated October 6, 1998.

CHAPTER THREE: ECONOMIC CRISIS

THE STORY OF the Great Recession starting in 2008 is based primarily on reports in *The Wall Street Journal*, *The New York Times* and *Washington Post*.

Professor Rips calculated the odds of "Economic Crisis," encoded just once in the Bible appearing with "the Depressions," also in the Bible only once, with the year it began 1929, and also 2012 as a million to 1.

Rips noted an interesting, and very likely intentional feature of the matrix: 1929 is followed by "year of," 2012 is followed by "it was shocked."

Federal Reserve Chairman Ben Bernanke stated it was "very likely" the recession had ended exactly one year after it began, *New York Times* September 15, 2009.

The Wall Street Journal article headlined "IS IT THE '30s' AGAIN?," was published on the 80th anniversary of the 1929 crash, October 18, 2009. The *Journal* noted that there were many "false dawns" in that ten year economic crisis.

The collapse of Lehman Brothers on September 15, 2008 seen by many as the beginning of the recession, was reported in the *Wall Street Journal*

September 15-16, 2008. Later, on December 29, 2008 the *Journal* recapped the crisis that followed in a story headlined "THE WEEKEND THAT WALL STREET DIED."

The official statement that the United States had been in a recession for a full year was announced December 1, 2008 by the National Bureau of Economic Research.

My letter to Obama's nominee to be Treasury Secretary, Timothy Geithner was sent the same day, and warned that the recession would last "at least four more years, until 2012." Geithner did not reply.

Obama's statement during the campaign that the economic crisis was the "final verdict" on the failed Republican free market philosophy, was reported in *The Washington Post* September 17, 2008.

General Motors went bankrupt June 1, 2009 and was front page news in *The Wall Street Journal* and *The New York Times* the next day.

Citigroup, once the world's biggest bank had to sell one-third of its stock to the government, *Wall Street Journal*, February to May, 2009.

The *Washington Post* story about Wall Street's crimes was published December 16, 2008.

Bernard Madoff was convicted of stealing $60 billion in a Ponzi scheme and sentenced to 150 years, reported in *The Wall Street Journal* June 30, 2009.

Goldman Sachs was sued for fraud by the Securities and Exchange Commission, reported in *The New York Times* April 16, 2010. On July 15 Goldman agreed to pay $550 million to settle the fraud case, the largest penalty any Wall Street firm ever paid the SEC, as reported by the *Times* and the *Wall Street Journal*. Goldman did not admit wrong-doing.

Obama's first address to Congress, assuring the country the economy would recover is quoted from a *New York Times* transcript February 24, 2009.

Nobel laureate economist Paul Krugman questioned Obama and Bernanke, stating, "This looks an awful lot like the beginning of a Great Depression," in his *New York Times* column January 5, 2009. In a later column Krugman said "things are still getting worse," *New York Times* April 17, 2009.

For a while in late 2009 and early 2010 Krugman backed off, saying a depression seemed unlikely, that instead we'd have a "jobless recovery." But when all of the major European countries started to slash spending, and Congress refused every attempt by Obama to stimulate a still feeble economy, Krugman once more declared, "We are now, I fear, in the early stages of a depression," *New York Times* June 27, 2010.

The great investor Warren Buffet was quoted as stating nuclear terror "is inevitable" by Allison (p. 14-15) and said something similar to *Fortune* magazine in an article dated November 11, 2002.

The *Newsweek* cover story "AMERICA'S BACK!" was published April 19, 2010.

The great flash crash of May 6, 2010, when the Dow Jones suddenly dropped almost 1000 points in minutes was reported in *The New York Times* and *Wall Street Journal* May 7, 2010.

In the summer of 2010 a stream of articles followed everywhere, the *Journal* and the *Times*, about the weak economy, a double-dip recession, maybe even a depression. *Time* magazine's July cover showed a chart with arrows pointing up and down, one labeled "economic crisis," the other "economic recovery."

No one knew, everyone was afraid.

CHAPTER FOUR: HEADLINE NEWS

PROFESSOR RIPS CALLED me from Israel on September 11, 2001, but could not reach me in New York the day of the attack, and we spoke September 12. It was then that he told me he had found every detail of 9/11 in the Bible Code, as I had, and also that the code had stated the correct death toll "about 3000."

Dr. Linton Wells, director of Command, Control, Communications, and Intelligence, the nerve center at the Pentagon, called me Sunday February 9, 2003 and told me that Deputy Secretary of Defense Paul Wolfowitz had asked me to brief the entire top military intelligence command about the Bible Code.

The meeting took place February 21, 2003, at 9AM, in the E ring of the Pentagon, the inner circle reserved for the Office of the Secretary of Defense.

The Admirals and Generals were focused on Iraq, which they were preparing to invade a month later. I said, "The real danger is not Saddam Hussein, but Osama bin Laden."

Al Qaeda's attack on the trains in Madrid March 11, 2004 was reported in *The New York Times* March 12. It was revenge for Spain's participation in our war in Iraq, and resulted in the fall of Spain's government, and its withdrawal from Iraq.

Al Qaeda's bombing of the London subway on July 7, 2005 was reported in *The New York Times* July 8. What shocked England as much as the murder of 52 people, was the fact that the terrorists were second generation Pakistanis, British citizens. Again it was blamed on England sending troops to Iraq.

The brazen terrorist attack on Mumbai, India by Pakistani militants closely tied to Al Qaeda on November 26, 2008 was reported in *The New York Times* November 27. Many suspected Pakistani intelligence was involved, because the three day siege was carried out with military precision.

Pakistani militants tied to Al Qaeda assassinated former Prime Minister Benazir Bhutto on December 27, 2008, and was reported in *The New York Times* December 28. Again many believed that Pakistani intelligence was involved in the murder of a leader who threatened to end years of military rule.

The most devastating recent natural disaster, the Asian Tsunami that killed 178,000 was reported in *The New York Times* December 27, 2004. The words of *The Times* report "wall of water" were exactly the same as the original words of the Bible that appeared where "Asia" and "Tsunami" crossed each other in the code.

The August 29, 2005 Hurricane Katrina that hit New Orleans and the next day flooded the city was reported in *The New York Times* August 30 and 31, and the days that followed. My account also relies on television coverage, mainly on CNN.

The January 12, 2010 earthquake in Haiti was reported in *The New York Times* January 13, and in the days that followed. The death toll was at least 200,000, perhaps even greater than the Asian Tsunami, but no true number is known for either disaster because so many were missing.

The Iceland volcano that covered the skies of the North Atlantic and most of Europe starting March 20, 2010 was reported in *The New York Times* March 21 and repeatedly in the days and weeks that followed, as there were further eruptions.

The April 20, 2010 explosion of the British Petroleum oil rig in the Gulf of Mexico was first reported in *The New York Times* April 21, and the coverage of the oil spill continued in all the major media for months. It is the worst ecological disaster in American history.

Climate change has been in the news for many years, but it was former Vice President Al Gore who more than anyone brought attention to what may become the world's most dangerous natural disaster. I relied on many media reports. The announcement of Gore's Nobel Prize was reported in *The New York Times* October 13, 2007.

I watched Obama's speech announcing he was sending 30,000 additional troops to Afghanistan on CNN on December 1, 2009, which was reported in *The New York Times* December 2. Both *The Times* and *Washington Post* reported that Vice President Biden opposed continuing the war President Bush launched in 2001, as did many Democrats in Congress.

CHAPTER FIVE: DENIAL

THE FAILED CHRISTMAS airplane bombing by a Nigerian trained by Al Qaeda in Yemen was reported in *The New York Times* December 26, 2009. Obama's outrage at the "systemic failure" of American intelligence was reported in *The New York Times* December 29.

John Brennan, the President's counter-terror advisor was assigned to investigate it, and according to a *Washington Post* story June 5, 2010, used his report to consolidate his control of U.S. intelligence by eliminating a rival nominally in charge, National Intelligence Director Adm. Dennis Blair.

What Obama did not know is that Brennan had for months ignored a warning of nuclear terror from Yemen. I first contacted him by fax December

30, 2009, and followed with a phone call January 3, 2010, telling Brennan that Israeli intelligence had confirmed the exact location of an Al Qaeda base that might be the hiding place for nuclear weapons.

General Yossi Kuperwasser, who confirmed the terrorist base in Yemen by satellite when he was Israel's chief intelligence analyst, gave the details to Brennan on January 11, 2010 through a CIA official Brennan sent from the American Embassy in Israel.

On March 5, 2010 I informed Brennan by fax that Kuperwasser would share the satellite photographs, but Brennan never made the necessary official request, and never again contacted Kuperwasser.

A year earlier, on January 16, 2009, right before Obama's Inauguration, I gave essentially the same information to Obama's transition chief John Podesta. After the failed Christmas bombing I called him to ask if he remembered the country I had named. "Yes, Yemen," Podesta replied, and he promised to contact Brennan and Obama's Chief of Staff Rahm Emanuel. Podesta never called either of them, nor did he call General Kuperwasser.

The May 1, 2010 failed Times Square bombing by a Pakistani who claimed he was trained by the Taliban, was reported in *The New York Times* May 2. Neither the underpants bomb worn by the Nigerian on Christmas, nor the Times Square SUV bomb exploded, but in neither case did American intelligence prevent it.

Nonetheless, Brennan quickly claimed the failure of the two terrorist attacks were a success for American intelligence, on CNN May 9, 2010.

Thomas Kean, Chairman of the 9/11 Commission, said the opposite: "The U.S. intelligence community is dysfunctional. We can't count on the terrorists being incompetent forever." (*Global Security Newswire*, June 1, 2010)

Professor Rips said something similar to me. "So the policy of American intelligence appears to be to hope that the terrorists are more incompetent than they are," he said. "This is not a good long-range plan."

Bin Laden and the Pakistani nuclear scientist Khan are encoded exactly where the name of the hideout for nuclear weapons also appears in the Bible. The same place name appears with "atomic" and "war."

I cannot tell the name in this book, because that would help the terrorists, and I cannot include the code matrixes that name the location in Yemen for the same reason, but I can state "Bin Laden" crosses it twice.

I first named the exact location to the CIA, U.S. military intelligence, and Israeli military intelligence at separate meetings, all in 2006. Israel confirmed the site in Yemen was an Al Qaeda base within weeks.

The quoted statement of a 9/11 Commission panel that Pakistan was the nexus of terrorism and nuclear weapons was published in an authorized edition of the report, *World at Risk* (Vintage Books, December 2008, p. xxiii).

The quote stating, "The next terrorist attack against the United States is likely to originate in Pakistan" is from the same report, p. xxiii.

General Kuperwasser, who confirmed the Al Qaeda base named in the code as Israel's top intelligence analyst, called Obama's counter-terror advisor Brennan at his White House office January 6, 2010. Brennan sent a CIA officer from the American Embassy in Israel to see Kuperwasser at his home January 11.

Kuperwasser told me a few hours after the meeting that he informed Brennan's emissary that the Bible Code had accurately named an Al Qaeda base confirmed by satellite and other classified means, that he gave the exact coordinates, and urged Brennan to contact me about the location of nuclear weapons.

In the same January 11 phone call, Kuperwasser said Israel would continue its search but that he was not certain his country could finish the job, that it might require the more advanced resources of U.S. intelligence.

I spoke to A.B. (Buzzy) Krongard, who had been Brennan's boss as Executive Director of the CIA, January 16, 2010, and he also urged Brennan to see me. Krongard called me March 1, after Brennan failed to meet with me or follow up with Kuperwasser, and said, "Tell the Israelis to give John the satellite photos. It's concrete evidence no one can ignore."

On March 3 I called Kuperwasser who told me Israel had found its original satellite photos from 2006, and took new satellite photos, but would need an official request from Brennan, an established procedure between Israeli and American intelligence.

On March 5, 2010 I faxed Brennan at the White House again, telling him what Kuperwasser had told me, telling him what Krongard had told me, and asking him, "Will you request the satellite photographs that prove the information I provided Israel is entirely accurate?"

Brennan never replied, he never contacted Kuperwasser, or even Krongard, and he never requested the satellite photographs. As this book was going to press September 7, 2010, Kuperwasser told me that the unit at Israeli military intelligence that confirmed the site had no record of any request from Brennan.

My entire account of the failure of American intelligence to prevent the 9/11 attacks, or to defend against them while they were happening on September 11, 2001, comes from *The 9/11 Commission Report* (Authorized Edition, W.W. Norton). I also witnessed the attack on the Twin Towers from the roof of my home in New York.

The quoted statement that Al Qaeda could attack the largest cities in the United States, is also from *The 9/11 Commission Report*, p. 362.

The quoted statement that "another catastrophic attack will materialize if the world's most dangerous terrorists acquire the world's most dangerous weapons," and that "Al Qaeda has tried to acquire or make nuclear weapons for at least ten years," are from the same report, p. 380.

The *New York Times* editorial "WHY DIDN'T THEY SEE IT?" about the failed Christmas bombing was published January 1, 2010.

America's secret funding of Bin Laden and Al Qaeda to fight the Soviets in Afghanistan is documented in *Ghost Wars*, Steve Coll (Penguin Books, 2005, pp. 89-93 and ff.).

Bush allowing Bin Laden to escape when he was trapped in his caves in the Tora Bora mountains in December 2001 is documented in *The Looming Tower*, Lawrence Wright (Knopf, 2006, p. 371).

Dr. Linton Wells, director of Command, Control, Communications, and Intelligence, the nerve center at the Pentagon, called me Sunday February 9, 2003 and told me that Deputy Secretary of Defense Paul Wolfowitz had asked me to brief the entire top military intelligence command about the Bible Code.

The meeting took place February 21, 2003, at 9AM, in the E ring of the Pentagon, the inner circle reserved for the Office of the Secretary of Defense. I stated the name of the Al Qaeda hideout, but did not yet know what country it was in, nor the years when nuclear weapons would be at the site.

I first met with Krongard, Executive Director of the CIA, on the same day of my 2003 Pentagon meeting. I called him after he retired in July 2006 and told him the Israelis had confirmed the Al Qaeda hideout in Yemen. He arranged my meeting with the new Deputy Director, Stephen Kappes.

I met with Kappes at CIA headquarters in Langley, Virginia July 26, 2006. Kappes' role in making a deal with Kaddafi to give up Libya's nuclear weapons program in 2003 is documented in *The Nuclear Jihadist*, Douglas Frantz and Catherine Collins (Twelve, 2007, p. 306 ff.). Kappes, the book reveals, relied heavily on British intelligence, and the CIA missed many opportunities to stop the man who sold Libya its bomb factory, the Pakistani nuclear smuggler Khan, over the previous three decades.

My account of the 2006 meeting with Kappes and his aides is documented by the notes I made during the meeting, and a memo I wrote right after I returned to New York.

Senator Edward Kennedy sent an official written request October 3, 2006 marked "URGENT" to the Director of National Intelligence John Negroponte, attaching a memo I sent Kennedy September 28.

My memo stated that Israeli intelligence had confirmed an Al Qaeda base in Yemen where nuclear weapons might exist, and that it told Kappes, who "apparently failed to take any action."

Kennedy's letter to Negroponte stated, "I received the attached correspondence yesterday from Michael Drosnin, who claims to have actionable intelligence about a potential immediate terrorist threat to America."

Kappes himself did not reply to Senator Kennedy but Negroponte would have had no other source for his reply, stating that the CIA had found no evidence to support my claim, which Kennedy's aide Joe Axelrad informed me of November 8, 2006.

A source close to Kappes told me that the CIA never tried to find any evidence, that it just ignored Israeli intelligence. General Kuperwasser confirmed his contact with Kappes' office, approved by the Prime Minister's military advisor.

I first met with General James Clapper on January 3, 2005 at the National Geospatial Intelligence Agency (NGA), in Bethesda, Maryland, where he was Director.

My account of our meeting is based on notes I made while I was with him, and on a memo I wrote when I returned to New York that night.

Clapper clearly took the Bible Code seriously, he met with me for two hours, from 2PM to 4PM, without taking a phone call. I told him that I had previously met with the Executive Director of the CIA, who told me that he had started the search, but that satellites, which worked very well in the Cold War, were practically useless in searching for small groups of terrorists or weapons that might be hidden in a tent in the desert.

"Oh, the Agency is a real mess now," said Clapper. "Besides, location is what we do, not the Agency. We're way better at it."

In fact, NGA was in charge of most of America's spy satellites, and Clapper told me he would immediately start a new search for the place the code named. Clapper assigned his top satellite analyst, Scott White, to the job.

White, however, was not able to find anything, including a related location I later found on Google Earth.

Clapper's question, "What if God wants to destroy the world?," came at the end of our meeting.

When I met with Clapper a second time at NGA, right before Thanksgiving, on November 23, 2005, he told me that his satellites had not yet confirmed an Al Qaeda base at either of the two locations with the same name in two countries. I did not yet know that the terrorist base was in Yemen.

It was at our second meeting that I showed Clapper a new set of code tables that persuaded him to keep looking—"America" encoded with "nuclear," and "atomic," and "terror," and "suicide bomber," against odds of at least 10 million to 1. Again, however, Clapper ended the meeting by saying, "But God might want the world to end."

On June 30, 2006 I met with Clapper's replacement at NGA, Acting Director Lloyd Rowland and his top satellite analyst White, who had been assigned the job originally by Clapper.

The Bible Code had just confirmed that the named Al Qaeda base was in Yemen and the code linked it to both Bin Laden and the Pakistani Khan, as I informed Clapper before he left NGA, May 30, 2006, in a fax from Israel.

Israeli intelligence confirmed the Al Qaeda base in Yemen by satellite in August 2006.

Clapper was named Undersecretary of Defense for Intelligence in 2007. I contacted him again at the Pentagon in September 2007, told Clapper that Israeli intelligence had confirmed the Al Qaeda base, and he asked me to meet with his deputy, Larry Burgess, America's chief military intelligence analyst.

Burgess and I met September 7, 2007, and I gave him a memo with new information from Israeli intelligence which confirmed that the Al Qaeda hideout was in Yemen, and that all the structures named in the code had been photographed by satellite.

Burgess was in charge of satellites and all other means of detection for the Pentagon, but he appeared not to comprehend the Bible Code tables I showed him, which now also named a mountain in which the nuclear weapons might be hidden. It appears that Burgess never followed through in any way.

Finally, on November 19, 2009, and again on December 30, 2009, after the failed Christmas bombing, I faxed Clapper, now chief of all military intelligence, telling him, "It's more important than ever now, because it's in Yemen"—the country where Al Qaeda had trained the bomber. Clapper never responded.

On June 5, 2010 President Obama nominated Clapper to be National Intelligence Director, in charge of all American Intelligence—the Pentagon, the CIA, NSA, all 16 agencies. It was reported the next day in the *New York Times* and *Washington Post*.

The Senate Intelligence Committee held confirmation hearings July 20, 2010, and questioned Clapper about a *Washington Post* expose that had appeared the day before stating that American intelligence had become so large and secretive that no one knew what it was doing, or if it worked. Clapper was quoted in the *Post* story July 19, as saying only God knew all of the secret intelligence programs.

The two year *Washington Post* investigation that was reported in a three part front page series, "TOP SECRET AMERICA," was published July 19, 20, and 21. It revealed that since 9/11 American intelligence had tripled in size and now had an annual budget of more than $75 billion - that Clapper himself admitted no human could see, let alone oversee.

"After nine years of unprecedented spending and growth," the *Post* said, "the result is that the system put in place to keep the United States safe is so massive that its effectiveness is impossible to determine."

The *Post* reported that:

- There are 1,271 government agencies, and 1,931 private companies doing counterterrorism work at 10,000 locations across the country.
- 854,000 people, one and a half times the population of Washington, had "top secret" security clearances.
- The private and government analysts published 50,000 reports every year, most routinely ignored because no one had time to read them.

Despite, or perhaps because of the size of the intelligence establishment, the *Post* noted, it was unable to stop a known terrorist on a "no fly" list from boarding an airplane with a bomb on Christmas 2009. He was prevented from igniting it by other passengers, not the government.

The agency that was supposed to connect the dots, to stop the underpants bomber or a future nuclear bomber, the National Counter-Terrorism Center, was originally created and directed by John Brennan, Obama's advisor who ignored the warning of nuclear terror from Yemen, even after Israeli intelligence confirmed the Al Qaeda base named in the Bible Code.

CHAPTER SIX: THE MOSSAD

My account of my March 20, 2009 meeting with General Meir Dagan, the Chief of the Mossad, is based on notes I made at the meeting and a memo I wrote immediately upon return to my hotel in Tel Aviv.

Dagan and I had met three times before, although he had never met with any other reporter. I was first introduced to Dagan by the chief scientist at the Ministry of Defense, General Isaac Ben-Israel.

At our first meeting on April 4, 2001, Dagan told me he had read my first *Bible Code* book when it was originally published in Hebrew in 1997, and that he believed it.

In fact, when we met a second time, December 4, 2001, Dagan told me he would talk to his close friend the Prime Minister, Ariel Sharon, and urge him to meet with me. At our third meeting on April 1, 2002, Dagan told me he had given Sharon a letter from me.

The day before I met with Dagan in March 2009, I first met with General Kuperwasser, the former chief analyst at Aman, Israel's military intelligence agency.

Kuperwasser told me he would confirm to Dagan that Aman had confirmed an Al Qaeda base in Yemen first named by the Bible Code, and every structure the code stated would be there.

A few days before the 2009 meeting, Professor Rips and I looked at the codes I would show Dagan. He confirmed their mathematical significance and also prepared a power-point presentation of the primary code matrix, "Bible Code" with "Bin Laden" and "Atomic," the Pakistani nuclear scientist "Khan," and "Yemen" against odds of 100 million to 1.

I first stumbled across the name of the Al Qaeda base many years earlier, and showed it to the military scientist General Ben-Israel in April 2002, noting that it appeared with nearly every encoding of great danger and every likely target.

Ben-Israel arranged for me to see General Kuperwasser, who I met with at the Kirya, Israeli military headquarters, on April 15, 2002. At that time, however, I did not know the base named in the code was in Yemen, I only knew the name of the base.

Finally, in June 2006 Professor Rips and I found the 100 million to 1 code matrix that revealed who, what, when, and where.

I met with Kuperwasser again in August 2006 and within two weeks Israel's one satellite found the base in Yemen. "It's an area of terrorist activity, it's Al Qaeda, and every structure the code said would be there is there," Kuperwasser told me.

He immediately arranged for me to see the Prime Minister's Military Secretary, General Gadi Shamni, who I met with August 17, 2006, despite the fact that Israel was in the middle of a war with Hezbollah in Lebanon and Hamas in Gaza.

Within days of the meeting Shamni briefed Shimon Peres, who was then Foreign Minister of Israel, and he also alerted all major military and intelligence officials.

However, at that time I only knew the code stated, "Starting 2006." It was years before I discovered that the Biblical year 5771, 2011 in the modern calendar, appeared in the same who, what, when, where matrix.

I told Professor Rips, and showed him that 2011 was overlapped in the code by "you will compute the time." Rips said, "This could not happen by chance. It is mathematically certain."

I told General Kuperwasser and then flew back to Israel to meet with the Chief of the Mossad General Dagan. Before I saw Dagan in March 2009, I met with Rips and two other famous Israeli scientists, Robert Aumann, a Nobel Laureate mathematician, and Yakir Aharonov, a physicist many expected to win a Nobel.

All three scientists told me the same thing: forget the 100 million to 1 odds of the code, all that mattered were the odds of it being confirmed by Israeli intelligence. All three top scientists agreed those odds were so great, they were beyond calculation.

And all three agreed that since everything Israel could see by satellite was confirmed, the one thing the satellite could not see - the nuclear weapons also stated in the code - had to be assumed real, unless proven false.

At our March 20, 2009 meeting, the Chief of the Mossad did not disagree. General Dagan simply stated, "It will be difficult to confirm the weapons."

I told him there were two ways Israel could confirm nuclear weapons were there—find them, and send in commandos to seize them, or wait until Israel, along with New York and Washington, were annihilated.

"What about the Americans?" asked Dagan.

I told him that American intelligence was broken, but that I hoped to see President Obama and CIA Director Leon Panetta. But I also warned Dagan not to depend on the United States to save Israel, that it was more likely Israel would save New York and Washington.

Dagan simply replied, "We have our ways."

CHAPTER SEVEN: WAR OF OBAMA

"War of Obama" is encoded in the Bible with "Saving the World," and the years 2011 and 2012, but I have no knowledge that the President himself expects, or wants such a war.

However, "War of Obama" is encoded with "terror" and so is "Huge War" and "World War."

And there is clear evidence that if Obama is not yet planning a global war on terror, the Pentagon is preparing for it.

The New York Times reported May 24, 2010 that General David Petraeus, "the top American commander in the Middle East, has ordered a broad expansion of clandestine military activity in an effort to disrupt militant groups or counter threats in Iran, Saudi Arabia, Somalia, and other countries in the region."

The *Times* stated he signed a secret directive September 30, 2009, authorizing U.S. Special Forces to operate in both friendly and hostile nations throughout the Middle East, Central Asia, and the Horn of Africa, to "pave the way for possible military strikes."

Officially called the Joint Unconventional Warfare Task Force Execute Order, the seven-page directive is aimed at destroying Al Qaeda, and authorizes specific operations in Iran and Yemen, the *Times* reported.

The article does not state Obama approved the directive, but he is Commander in Chief, and no General would have issued such a sweeping order without the President's knowledge.

Obama's statement that "the risk of nuclear attack has gone up," which he specifically linked to Al Qaeda, came in a speech he made in Prague on April 5, 2009, during his first trip abroad as President, reported in *The New York Times* and *Washington Post* April 6.

The President's bomb shelter, Raven Rock, is also an "underground Pentagon" buried deep inside a mountain, 6 miles from Camp David, and was first revealed in detail by James Bamford, *Pretext for War,* (Anchor Books, 2005, p. 77 ff.). It was created at the height of the Cold War to fight a nuclear war from underground, but was also used by Vice President Dick Cheney in the aftermath of 9/11.

The plan for a "unilateral strike in Pakistan" was revealed in *The Washington Post* May 29, 2010.

The same story quoted Secretary of State Hillary Clinton, after the failed Times Square bombing by a Pakistani, as saying that a successful terrorist attack traced to Pakistan would result in "very severe consequences."

No one quoted in the *Post* story suggested what America would do if the terrorist attack was nuclear, or spoke of a pre-emptive strike.

However, the leading expert on nuclear terror, Graham Allison, stated, "Detonated in Times Square a ten-kiloton weapon could kill one million New Yorkers" (*Nuclear Terrorism*, p. 204).

The *Post* story May 29, 2010, did state that Obama sent his National Security Advisor Gen. Jones and CIA Director Panetta to state the consequences to Pakistani leaders, including the military chief, General Ashfaq Kiyani who was director of Pakistani intelligence and is now its military chief. He also controls Pakistan's 100 nuclear weapons, so the same intelligence organization which helped create Al Qaeda now controls the weapons.

The statement that half of all nuclear weapons and enriched uranium in the world is now vulnerable to terrorists was made by Allison, p. 60–86.

Allison also stated that to prevent nuclear terrorism we must "prevent terrorists from acquiring nuclear weapons," p. 15.

In the same book, Allison, the leading expert, stated that "covert and overt military force" might be necessary to achieve that goal, p. 157.

"On the current course, nuclear terror is inevitable," wrote Allison, p. 203.

Every expert on nuclear terror agrees that if we allow one city to be annihilated, there will be, as Allison states, a "cascade of nuclear weapons exploding in our cities," that would "destroy civilization as we know it," p. 191, 220.

CHAPTER EIGHT: SAVING THE WORLD

THE IMAGE OF President Obama receiving the Nobel Peace Prize December 10, 2009 in Oslo, Norway, was captured the same day in television network reports, and reported in *The New York Times* December 11.

The quoted statement of the Nobel Chairman, Thorbjorn Jagland, invoking Martin Luther King was reported in the *Times*.

Obama's full 36-minute speech accepting the prize appeared in a transcript also in the *Times*, December 11.

The President's statement that shocked the Nobel audience, that the world had to embrace the concept of a "just war," was reflected in the *Times'* headline "ACCEPTING PEACE PRIZE, OBAMA OFFERS 'HARD TRUTH'."

The danger of nuclear terrorism was central to Obama's speech, and the reason why he stated the world "will find the use of force not only necessary but morally justified."

Professor Rips confirmed that the encoding in the Bible of "Obama Nobel" with "his prize" "peace" was "perfect, remarkable, and absolutely beyond chance."

Rips also confirmed the code matrix in which "Saving the World" appears with "Obama will make real," and was not surprised to see that it also stated, "With a code."

Biblical years can be written in Hebrew letters, because every letter in the Hebrew alphabet is also a number. So the year in the modern calendar 2010, in the Biblical calendar 5770, written in letters also spells a question, "Will you save?"

The Bible Code consistently predicts Obama will "save the world," although perhaps in 2011 or 2012, and specifically against the threat of "atomic weapons."

But as I told Obama in the letter I sent him through Oprah, which stated that he could as President prevent an otherwise inevitable nuclear terror attack, also made clear that everything in the Bible Code is a probability, not a determined fact, therefore a destiny he would have to fulfill.

Professor Rips' statement that the one reason he believed the world would survive was "God's promise after the Flood never to destroy the world again," was stated to me when I met with him in mid March 2009, while preparing to see the Chief of the Mossad.

The quoted passages from the Bible Rips referenced are God's promise to Noah after the Flood, in Genesis 9:11-17.

My unexpected discovery that the only encoding of "Changing the Future" appeared with the exact passage in Genesis Rips quoted was a total surprise, a code matrix I found while I was finishing writing this book more than a year later.

The alternative theory of Carl Sagan that all intelligent species everywhere in the universe would create the means to destroy themselves, and then eventually do it, was stated by Sagan in *Cosmos* (Random House, 1980, p. 318).

The opposite theory, that we can use our free will to survive, comes from an ancient commentary on the Bible, The Talmud, and is attributed to Rabbi Akiva (*Mishna Avot* 3:15).

Rips' statement that for the Encoder all time is simultaneous, the past, present, and future, was stated to me in our same March 2009 meeting.

Einstein's similar statement that "past, present, and future" are one, was made on March 21, 1955, and published in *The Quotable Einstein* (Princeton University Press, 1996, p. 61)

My entire conversation with Rips in this chapter about survival, free will, and how the future could be changed, took place at his home in Jerusalem in the same series of meetings in mid-March 2009.

"He will change the future," appears in the code with "in the End of Days" and "peace," and was again confirmed by Rips when I found it a year later as being beyond chance.

The apparent contradiction between a good outcome and "in the End of Days" is resolved by the original Hebrew, which can be read in two ways, the end of the world, but also instead, "in the Latter Days," our own era, the future foreseen 3000 years ago, which we can change.

However, the code repeatedly links Obama saving the world to a "battle," to "a very great blow," to "war."

Even "World Peace" appears with "all his people to war," suggesting that what the President stated in accepting the Nobel Peace Prize, that peace would need to be achieved through war, is correct.

The "War of Obama" encoded in the Bible, that the *New York Times* reported May 24, 2010, was being planned by the Pentagon since September 2009 is no longer just a plan.

On June 4, 2010 *The Washington Post* revealed that U.S. Special Forces are already deployed in 75 countries.

"Plans exist for pre-emptive or retaliatory strikes in numerous places around the world," the *Post* stated in the same story.

My greatest concern was that the clearest statement of the secret war in progress came from the same White House counter-terror advisor who refused to even see the evidence Israeli intelligence offered him about a confirmed Al Qaeda base in Yemen, that the Bible Code stated as the hideout for nuclear weapons.

Brennan told the *Post* the United States "will not merely respond after the fact to a terrorist attack," but will "take the fight to Al Qaeda whether they plot and train in Afghanistan, Pakistan, Yemen, and beyond."

A covert war in 75 countries will not prevent the most immediate danger of nuclear terror. Only a focused pre-emptive attack on the known Al Qaeda base in Yemen, after the exact location of the nuclear weapons is confirmed, will save New York, Washington, Israel, and finally all of human civilization.

Obama can only fulfill his destiny to save the world if his closest advisors actually do what the President himself has promised.

CODA

I DID NOT seek out the "Code Key" while working on this book. The Bible Code itself, however, kept drawing me back to the key, stating it was "the solution" to the "Atomic Terror Attack" threatened by "Bin Laden."

It suggested over and over again, until I could not ignore it, that the key to the code was also the key to our survival.

No matter what I looked for, whether it was a prediction of Obama's election, or the danger of a nuclear terror attack, the key and its location, a peninsula that juts out into the Dead Sea from Jordan, named "Lisan," kept appearing in the matrix.

My 12 year effort to launch an archeological expedition to dig up the Code Key started in May 1998 in Rips' home in Jerusalem. He told me we would never be able to see the code completely unless we found its key.

"Even using the most powerful computers we possess today, we cannot solve its mystery," he said, "until the key to the code is found."

Rips' email confirming that "Code Key" twice crossed "Obelisks" against odds of a million to 1 was sent January 2, 2002.

A 1700 year old Midrash states the "Obelisks" "were not what a human being had made, but the work of Heaven." It also suggests the Obelisks are humanoid, "a kind of male and female." *Mekhilta According to Rabbi Ishmael, An Analytical Translation* (trans. Jacob Neusner, Scholars Press, 1988).

For two years I planned the expedition to Lisan talking with Biblical scholars and geologists, and finally visited the peninsula in November 1998 and returned there in March and April 1999 with archeologists, geologists, geophysicists. I went back on February 16, 2000 accompanied by officials from Jordan's Ministry of Tourism and Antiquities.

Two days earlier on February 14, 2000 I had met in Amman with its Minister, Akel Biltaji, and he assured me I would receive the necessary permit for an archeological survey. The written permit dated April 13, 2000 was granted by the Director of the Department of Antiquities, Dr. Fawwaz Al-Khraysheh.

But just as the expedition was about to go forward Minister Biltaji refused to let me exercise the permit he had granted. There was no explanation.

But at the same time a Jordanian newspaper *Al-Arab Al-Yawm* published a front page attack on the archeological dig on January 9, 2001. Almost every statement in the story was untrue, but the basic message was clear: "Why would a Jewish foundation be allowed to dig for Jewish artifacts on Jordanian territory?"

The American Ambassador to Jordan, William Burns, immediately intervened with Biltaji and later with Saleh Rusheidat, Deputy Prime Minister of Jordan, but also cautioned, "There is a blacklist against anyone who has contact with Jews here."

I said that the new young King of Jordan, Abdullah II, had openly spoken out against the blacklist but Burns cautioned against any immediate effort to contact the King. "He's in a very difficult position," said the Ambassador. "He's Bedouin and most of his population is Palestinian."

The Ambassador finally did try to arrange for me to meet with King Abdullah, as did succeeding American Ambassadors, but to no avail.

I was always certain that if the King would see me he would allow me to go forward, indeed, would help. I wrote to him several times giving as references everyone from Shimon Peres to Yasir Arafat, both of whom had met with me, and knew me as a friend of peace. The King's father, Hussein, had made peace with Israel, one of only two Arab leaders to do so. But it appeared that my letters never reached his son.

I now believe that only a call from the White House, perhaps only from the President himself, to King Abdullah will enable me to exercise the permit I've had for 10 years, and perhaps find the key to the code that Obama may need to save the world.

APPENDIX

APPENDIX

THE 2012 PRESIDENTIAL election may be a contest between Barack Obama and Sarah Palin.

The Bible Code repeatedly states it as a possibility, although it is too soon to be certain.

But so many people have asked me the question, usually in horror of a possible President Palin, but sometimes in fear or favor of Obama's re-election, that I finally did search the code.

Here is a preview of the possible 2012 race for the White House, from the Bible Code.

"Obama" and "Palin" cross each other only once, and "Obama" is clearly the victor—his name is overlapped by "he was elected."

O PALIN △ OBAMA ◇ HE WAS ELECTED

The code is emphatic in stating Obama's victory over Palin—"truth they confirmed" crosses his name and "he was elected."

שׁ מ ו ל א י ז ע ן ב ן פ צ י ל א י ת ה ק ה ת ח פ שׁ מ ל ב א
ס י פ ל א ת שׁ שׁ ה ל ע מ ו שׁ ד ח ן ב מ ר כ ז ל כ ו פ ס מ ב
ע ו מ ל ה א י נ פ ל ה מ ד ק ן כ שׁ מ ה י נ (פ) ל ס י נ ח ה ו
מ ת א א שׁ ו ה ל ע מ ו שׁ ד ח ן ב מ ל א ו שׁ (י) י נ ב ל ו כ ז
ו ס י ע ב שׁ ו ה שׁ ל שׁ ף ל א ס י ו שׁ ע ו ס (ו) נ שׁ ס ה י ד ק
ס י ו שׁ ע ח ק ת שׁ ד ק ה ל ק שׁ ב ת ל ג ל ג (ל) ס י ל ק שׁ ת שׁ
א ٭ ו ה י ה ו צ ו שׁ [א] כ ٭ ו ה י י פ ל ע ו (ו) נ ב ל ו נ ו ה
א ו ד ⟨ו⟩ ו |ה| ו ה נ ⟨ח⟩ |מ| ה ע ס נ ⟨ב⟩ ו י נ ב נ |ה| ⟨ח⟩ ר ה א |א| ב ו ס
ט כ ו י נ שׁ ת ע ל ו |ת| ד ג ב ס ה י ל ע ו שׁ ו פ ו ה י ה י ו
ר ו ע ה ס כ מ ב ו נ ת |א| ו ס ו ו ת ל כ ת ד ג ב ו שׁ ו פ י ב ה
כ ת ק ו ז מ ה ת א ו |ס| י ע י ה ת א ו ת ג ל ז מ ה ת א ת ת ה
ת ח נ מ ו ס י מ ס ה ה |ת| ו ט ק ו ר ו א מ ה ו מ שׁ ו ה כ ה ו ר
א ל ו ו א שׁ מ ל א ו |ו| ת ד ב ע ל ע שׁ י א שׁ י א ס ת ו א ו מ
מ ה ת ע י ר י ת א ו א נ שׁ ו ו א שׁ מ ל ו ד ב ע ל י ו ג שׁ ו ג ה
ל י נ שׁ ו ג ה י נ ב ת ד ב ע ל כ ה י ה ת ו י נ ב ו ו ר ה א

O PALIN   △ OBAMA   ⬠ HE WAS ELECTED   ☐ TRUTH THEY CONFIRMED

But the very fact that "Palin" crosses "Obama" does suggest she may be his opponent.

Obama is likely to win a second term no matter who runs against him. The year of the next election, 2012, appears in two of the same code matrixes that predicted Obama would be elected in 2008—both found a year before he won.

"B. Obama is President" appears with "starting 2012." The year is encoded right between "Obama" and "experienced President."

"Starting 2012" obviously refers to his running a second time, as does "experienced President."

"The Obama codes are remarkable and could not appear by chance," said Professor Rips. "Even this one matrix is extraordinary."

O B. OBAMA IS PRESIDENT   □ EXPERIENCED PRESIDENT

▽ OBAMA   ◇ STARTING 5772 / 2012   △ NOVEMBER

"Obama will be elected" is also encoded with "President" and "in 2012."
"He will win" appears with a phrase that may explain how and why, "He ran
for national security."

Everything stated in the code makes it appear the 2012 election may, in
fact, be about the "War of Obama," the war that might be necessary to prevent nuclear terror.

Obama would then run as a wartime President.

O OBAMA WILL BE ELECTED   □ PRESIDENT

☐ HE RAN FOR NATIONAL SECURITY   ◇ HE WILL WIN   ◇ IN 5772 / 2012

Finally, "re-elected" appears with "Obama" "sworn in twice."

That matrix seems to leave little room for doubt. It is an explicit statement that the President will get 4 more years. As unlikely as that may look right now, it is certainly more likely than his improbable victory in 2008.

O RE-ELECTED   △ OBAMA   □ SWORN IN TWICE

"In war room" is encoded in the same matrix, indeed it appears three times, suggesting we may indeed be at war in 2012.

O RE-ELECTED   △ OBAMA   □ SWORN IN TWICE   O WAR ROOM   O WAR ROOM

O IN WAR ROOM

If we are in the middle of a major war against terrorism in 2012, the voters may well decide, as they usually do, not to risk changing the Commander-in-Chief. Obama would from a "war room" run "for national security," and win the election.

But despite all the encodings of a second term for Obama, there does appear to be at least the chance of a different outcome.

"Palin" is twice crossed by "President." Indeed, "President" is encoded five times in the same matrix.

When I first saw it, I was surprised. "President Palin" suddenly seemed a very real possibility.

O PALIN   □ PRESIDENT   □ PRESIDENT   □ PRESIDENT
□ PRESIDENT   □ PRESIDENT

But Palin's apparent victory is not really stated in the code. "President," as it appears all five times, can only be a man.

In Hebrew, as in most languages, the title must be in a female form if the President is a woman.

And a woman as President never appears against high odds with Sarah Palin.

It is encoded once with "S. Palin," but not in a mathematically meaningful way, just 50 to 1. Professor Rips stated, "It is not enough to suggest she will be President."

O S. PALIN   △ PRESIDENT

Sarah Palin may not even be a footnote in American history, may not be the Republican candidate, or even a Tea Party candidate.

But she appears in the Bible Code in a way that suggests it's a real possibility that she will run—but lose.

O S. PALIN   ☐ SARAH   △ SHE WILL BE SELECTED   ☐ FAILURE

"S. Palin" appears with "Sarah" and "she will be selected." But "failure" is encoded in exactly the same place.

And the odds of "Palin" and "selected" being in the same matrix are only 20 to 1. "It is not striking," said Rips.

Palin may be "selected" as a candidate in 2012 the code suggests—but not "elected" President.

There are so many unknowns two years in advance of the 2012 race that the outcome cannot really be found, not definitively.

We do not yet know who will be running, and must know the names of all the candidates to do a real search in the code.

We do not yet know if a predicted "Economic Crisis," perhaps the second Great Depression stated as a probability in the code will actually happen. Or if that will make voters want to stay with a known leader, as they did four times with Roosevelt, or switch to a radical outsider.

We do not yet know if a predicted "War of Obama" will happen in 2011 or 2012, or may be avoided by a pre-emptive strike that stops nuclear terror attacks on New York and Washington. If they are not prevented, there may be no election in 2012.

If Obama does prevent the danger, if he seizes weapons Al Qaeda may already have, then it is certain he will win, likely in the biggest landslide in American history, no matter who else runs.

ACKNOWLEDGEMENTS

ACKNOWLEDGEMENTS

THIS BOOK, AS the prior two in the Bible Code trilogy, is based on decades of extraordinary work by an internationally respected Israeli mathematician who discovered the code, a great scientist who is now my good friend Eli Rips.

Ever since I first met him in June 1992 we have spoken often, and met many times. The evidence that the Bible Code is real came from many sources, but this book could not have been written without Professor Rips' constant help, and profound insights.

It was written independently of him, however, and the views expressed in it are mine, not his, except for his quoted remarks.

I used the computer program he created with his colleague Dr. Alex Rotenberg for all my code research. The published matrixes were made using software he developed with Dr. Alex Polishuk.

Many American and Israeli government officials helped in many important ways. I won't thank them all by name, because that might make their jobs more difficult. But I must thank my friend General Yossi Kuperwasser, who until recently was the chief intelligence analyst in Israel.

It was Yossi who personally confirmed by satellite and other means that a dot in the desert named in the code was in fact an area of Al Qaeda activity, with every structure stated in the code. And it is Yossi who is still working to get American and Israeli intelligence to finish the job, to find and capture the nuclear weapons Al Qaeda may already have.

Oprah Winfrey played a vital role in getting my letter to Barack Obama, when he was still a candidate, predicting that he would be President, but also warning of two dangers. It took unusual courage to send her friend Obama predictions based on a code in the Bible that revealed the future, but Oprah did not hesitate to do it.

The President's closest friend and advisor, Valerie Jarrett, alerted the Secret Service to the second prediction, that Obama's life might be in danger, but that he could, perhaps with the help of the code, be saved.

Several friends took time to read, criticize, and encourage. One, Jon Larsen, did far more. His advice has always been both bold and intelligent, as it has been for every book I've ever written.

Another friend, my attorney Ken Burrows, a true author's lawyer, helped in ways that went well beyond legal advice.

Many publishers and editors in many countries helped bring this book to the world. I must especially thank my British editor, Ion Trewin, who is literary director of his country's most prestigious literary award, the Booker Prize. He has been my editor from the start of the Bible Code series, and his advice and support have always been extraordinary.

The Perseus Books Group made this book possible to publish independently in the United States, as I've long wanted. I thank its CEO David Steinberger, Sabrina McCarthy, and Matty Goldberg. Without Perseus, there would be no independent publishing in America.

I must also thank Chip Kidd, the artist who created the jacket for the U.S. edition, as he did for the first two. Pauline Neuwirth, the interior designer, produced a book in record time, with the skilled and tireless assistance of Sean Bellows.

This book would not have been possible without the help of several assistants, especially Yifat and Shelly. These two young Israelis not only confirmed the translations, but also were the first readers of my work in progress, helping me in every way. I would not have made it without them.

INDEX

INDEX

NOTE: Boldface page numbers refer to illustrated Bible Code printouts.

A B O U T   T H E   A U T H O R

MICHAEL DROSNIN is a reporter, formerly at the Washington Post and the Wall Street Journal. He is the author of three New York Times bestsellers, *Citizen Hughes*, *The Bible Code*, and *Bible Code II: The Countdown*. He lives and works in New York City.